The

THE PRACTICE OF *A COURSE IN MIRACLES*

The Arch of Forgiveness

KENNETH WAPNICK, Ph.D.

Foundation for A COURSE IN MIRACLES®

Foundation for A Course in Miracles®
41397 Buecking Drive
Temecula, CA 92590
www.facim.org

First printing, 2006

Printed in the United States of America

Library of Congress Cataloging-in-Publication Data

Wapnick, Kenneth, 1942-
The arch of forgiveness : the practice of A course in miracles / Kenneth Wapnick.
p. cm.
Includes bibliographical references and index.
ISBN 13: 978-1-59142-210-5
ISBN 10: 1-59142-210-8
1. Course in miracles. I. Title.
BP605.C68W3582 2005
299'.93--dc22 2005035473

CONTENTS

Preface

This book is derived from a number of different classes held at the Foundation, unified by the theme of contrasting life within and without the arch of peace, its pillars framed by Jesus and his message of forgiveness. The image of the arch was drawn from D. H. Lawrence's novel *The Rainbow*, as is explained in Chapter 2, and expresses the safety and peace found when one chooses Jesus as one's teacher instead of the ego.

The two chapters that follow the Introduction present our theme of the arch: Jesus' arch of safety and love, and the ego's unsafe arch of the body. The fourth chapter contrasts the song of the ego's child with the song of the Child Who lives in all of us, and ends with a discussion of the real world, based on the section from the text, "The Forgiving Dream." The final chapter consists of question and answers from other classes and workshops. These augment the discussion of the first two chapters through exploring the practical applications of the principles of living under the arch.

It should also be mentioned that one of the classes was held at a time when a hurricane was striking the southern states where some of the participating students had their homes, and so part of the discussion focused on their obvious concerns and the issues raised by the storm.

As with other books in this series, we have attempted to keep the atmosphere of informality of the classes themselves. To this end, our editing sought to preserve the spirit of the spoken word as opposed to the more polished written word, as well as inserting several questions that reflect the classroom setting. On the level of content, this little book has as its aim to reinforce in its readers the desire for a life of forgiveness, for only within Jesus' arch can true happiness come as we—together with him and all our brothers—make our way up the spiritual ladder and return home.

Acknowledgments

Rosemarie LoSasso, our Director of Publications has once again done a stellar job of organizing and editing the material for yet another book, for which I am very grateful. I should also like to express loving gratitude to my wife Gloria, who for almost twenty-five years has faithfully shared my life as we have together striven to live as one under Jesus' arch of forgiveness and love.

1. Introduction

Our Lives as Classrooms

One of the most important shifts students of *A Course in Miracles* can make is to regard their lives as classrooms, and to accept that they are minds choosing to learn lessons from either Jesus or the ego. When we speak of viewing our lives this way, we speak of a shift in how we look at everything. Indeed, a miracle can be defined as a shift in perception—from the ego's way of looking, to the Holy Spirit's. Then, too, if our lives are classrooms, we are constantly learning, and the crucial issue becomes *who* is it who learns, as reflected in the question Jesus poses near the beginning of the text: "Who is the 'you' who are living in this world?" (T-4.II.11:8). We can rephrase the question: Who is the "you" who are *learning* in this world?

Thus, we cannot truly learn from Jesus and benefit from his course unless we accept that it is the mind, not the body, that learns—what we term *the decision maker*. If we believe the body learns, our lives will revolve around our physical and psychological needs, and our learning will be focused on how best to satisfy them. As minds, however, our learning focuses on "unlearning," which is how Jesus characterizes *true learning* (M-4.X.3:7). The decision-making part of the mind learns to unlearn its mistaken choice for the ego. We have to be taught that when we chose the ego, we were taught falsely and therefore learned insane lessons that do not make us happy or peaceful. These lessons do not end suffering, and do not grant us eternal life. Our teacher Jesus thus wants us to question why we continually choose the ego, when it is the one thing that does not know what has to be taught; in fact, it knows nothing at all and only means us ill.

Many times in *A Course in Miracles*—implicitly and explicitly—Jesus asks us to orient our day in terms of purpose. As soon as we awaken, he asks us to think about its purpose as a classroom, and then to reaffirm this at night when we go to sleep. In Lesson 61, for example, he says:

> Be sure both to begin and end the day with a practice period. Thus you will awaken with an acknowledgment of the truth about yourself, reinforce it throughout the day, and turn to sleep as you reaffirm your function and your only purpose here (W-pI.61.6:1-2).

Our day is therefore not about having our needs met. Whenever we start worrying about something—a relationship, business meeting, or doctor's appointment—we have forgotten the day's purpose. Even looking forward to the day tells us we have forgotten its purpose. If we are honest, we will acknowledge that our concerns focus primarily on ourselves as physical and emotional bodies. If we identify with other people's bodies and feel concern for them, it is psychologically the same thing—a red flag alerting us that we have forgotten the day's purpose of being a classroom for learning. Recalling this purpose shifts the focus from apprehension or excitement to seeing that whatever happens, it is an opportunity for learning more about the ego. We act appropriately, doing what normal people do, but a part of us will observe how we carry out the real purpose of the day's events and situations: to see how quickly we are tempted to return to the ego, lose our peace, and blame another for it. And so we learn we can be at peace, regardless of what occurs outside. This will remain our focus as long as we remember we are always in class, and always choosing our teacher.

The Introduction to the fourth review in the workbook reflects this approach:

> We add no other thoughts, but let these be the messages they are. [The message of the review is "My mind holds only what I think with God."] We need no more than this to give us happiness and rest, and endless quiet, perfect certainty, and all our Father wills that we receive as the inheritance

> we have of Him. Each day of practicing, as we review, we close as we began, repeating first the thought that made the day a special time of blessing and of happiness for us; and through our faithfulness restored the world from darkness to the light, from grief to joy, from pain to peace, from sin to holiness (W-pI.rIV.in.9).

Thus we begin and end the day in remembrance of who we are.

This is a constant instruction throughout the workbook because Jesus wants us to shift the focus of our day while we continue our normal behavior. We take care of our bodies and those of loved ones; we provide for ourselves and others; we work and play. Yet we do not forget that our lives are not about the body—a vehicle we made for the purpose of attack and separation—which Jesus uses as a learning device to bring our attention back to the mind. We are not here to save or heal the world, to take care of ourselves or loved ones, but to learn. The world is our classroom, and it is helpful to see how quickly we forget, allowing the body to assume front-and-center stage.

Indeed, this is the body's purpose. Bodies dominate our lives, for they scream: *Me, me, me*—serve me, stroke me, attack me, love me; above all, pay attention to me. A clever but highly effective ego maneuver is to make the body so repulsive that we will be rejected and ignored. After all, the world would not hate us so much, nor shun us if it did not first notice us. Thus the ego will get us any which way—whether we are nice people everyone loves to be with, or so terrible that everyone avoids us. Loved or hated, what matters is only that we are noticed.

We will discuss later how the approach of framing our days as classrooms provides a safe, protected, and wonderful environment, within which nothing external can truly hurt us since it is only the mind that learns. In the concluding section of the teachers' manual, "As for the Rest … ," Jesus assures us that we will benefit greatly from such framing and asking the Holy Spirit's help:

> If you have made it a habit to ask for help when and where you can, you can be confident that wisdom will be given you when you need it (M-29.5:8).

This wisdom is not about which job to take, what relationship to be in, or where to live, but a wisdom that helps us realize that nothing here makes any difference. Moreover, we learn that everything that happens is a device to help us reach the place of peace inside us.

Jesus therefore wants us to:

> Prepare for this each morning, remember God when you can throughout the day, ask the Holy Spirit's help when it is feasible to do so, and thank Him for His guidance at night. And your confidence will be well founded indeed (M-29.5:9-10).

In a sense, this is *A Course in Miracles'* alpha and omega—the beginning and end—and healing is fostered by our seeing how quickly we try to move away from this simple truth, and then forgive ourselves.

2. The Arch of Safety and Love

Seeing our day within the framework of a classroom guarantees our learning. This not only makes the day meaningful, but also provides comfort and security. There is a moving account of this in a remarkable passage in D. H. Lawrence's *The Rainbow*, one of the twentieth century's most beautifully written novels. Unfortunately, this British author is more widely known for *Lady Chatterly's Lover*, hardly one of his better works. *The Rainbow* was Lawrence's fourth book, written when he was only 28. It is striking that one so young had such profound insight into relationships, more so than any writer I have read, and thus shocking to think that such a beautiful and sensitive book was banned in England on charges of obscenity.

The story covers three generations. The first, Tom and Lydia Brangwen, came from different cultures, and their marriage was quite rocky. Lydia came to Tom with a daughter from a previous marriage, whose name was Anna. Lawrence portrays the healing of Tom and Lydia's relationship, and although the word does not appear in this context, they *forgive* the differences, resulting in a genuinely deep bond between them. Lawrence then describes Anna, her parents having healed their rift, thus becoming pillars of strength supporting her little life:

> Her soul was put at peace between them. She looked from one to the other and she saw them established to her safety, and she was free. She played between the pillar of fire and the pillar of cloud in confidence, having the assurance on her right hand and the assurance on her left. She was no longer called upon to uphold with her childish might the broken end of the arch. Her father and her mother now met to the span of the heavens, and she, the child, was free to play in the space beneath, between.*

The image of the arch transmutes to a rainbow later in the novel, and indeed, the book ends with this image. I have always been struck by the above passage, because the core of a good family is that children no longer feel they have to support the broken end of the parental arch, which devastates them as they are almost inevitably forced to buy into the pathology of the relationship and uphold one parent or the other. In this instance, however, the parents' love for each other became the arch that framed young Anna's life, freeing her to grow within the arch of love that became an arch of safety for her.

---

* D. H. Lawrence, *The Rainbow* (Wordsworth Editions Ltd, Hertfordshire, UK, 1995), p.79.

Many passages in *A Course in Miracles* reflect the same idea. Jesus wants us to feel the safety a child feels when protected by the love that surrounds it. We cannot grow, however, if we do not have the freedom to be a child, and do not experience the security that allows us to grow without assuming adult responsibility. Moreover, when we identify with the body and our day focuses on satisfying its needs, we are burdened with a great sense of responsibility. We try to make others responsible, but the truth is that *we* are responsible for trying to make others responsible. Yet when we live in our right minds, our only responsibility is to remain within the arch—the loving framework that Jesus, our older brother, offers us.

To extend the metaphor of the arch, we could say that the two pillars are forgiveness and the teacher of forgiveness, framing our daily lives if we so choose. Within its pillars of safety, we have the freedom to grow as minds, no longer identifying with a vulnerable body that is under constant threat. No safety or security can exist within the body, which is continually buffeted around; its needs met one minute, which then return the next, or else different needs arise. When we identify with the mind—the decision maker as learner—and learn the principle of forgiveness from the teacher of love, we are safe, and nothing that happens around us could ever hurt us. Regardless of world events—collective or personal—we remain safe because we remain within the arch. When we step outside, however—leaving the mind and fleeing to the body and its dream—we lose our happiness, because none exists outside the arch.

In his course, Jesus helps us remain within the arch that is our classroom. Recalling his statement from the text, "The ark of peace is entered two by two" (T-20.IV.6:5), we can know it as the arch of peace. Another lovely image is the "little garden," into which we welcome others (T-18.VIII). Yet must we invite *everyone* to join us there, including all we would seek to exclude, for in excluding even one person, we exclude ourselves. No one rests in the arch of peace alone. We are there with everyone, or not there at all. When we exclude, we catapult ourselves outside the arch and so become vulnerable, existing in a threatening and hostile world in which there is no hope, except to find ways to survive. In this way we focus again on our physical and psychological needs, inevitably leading us to cannibalize, seduce, manipulate, judge, or kill. Thus does peace inevitably disappear from our awareness.

Over time we become so sensitive to the loss of peace that the minute it happens, we quickly return to the arch and to the teacher who teaches us a different way of looking at the world. He helps us see that the threat does not come from the outside, nor does salvation come from judgment. Everything then changes. It is a question only of which arch we choose to be under: the ego's, which is not protective at all, or Jesus', where we have the freedom to be the child—not the unruly child of the temper tantrum, but the child that says: "I want to learn and grow, so one day I can be a pillar." In effect, we grow adjacent to Jesus' loving pillar of forgiveness, so that when we grow up, we fuse into that pillar, becoming the gentle strength that welcomes everyone to come within its embrace. To achieve this happy state is how we should see the purpose of our days.

Whenever anything disrupts our peace, we know we have left the arch, and then all hell breaks loose. However, we need only come back and peace will return, for within the pillars of safety, we know that nothing outside them can affect us. We remain aware of what goes on, but realize it has no power to take away our peace or give it to us. The world thus has no power to make us happy or sad, which removes the tremendous burden of having to judge and evaluate: this is a good person, this is a bad one; this is a good thing, this is a bad one. Within the arch, there is no good or bad. Everyone and everything rests within its pillars of safety, which means differences are meaningless. Whenever we do not feel safe, and are anxious, angry, depressed, or sick, it is because we stepped out from under the arch. We need know nothing else. The answer to our problems, then, is simple: we return to our home, there to live, grow, and recognize that suffering comes from giving power to the world outside—yet there *is* nothing outside.

Thus is my mind healed, as forgiveness and Jesus become the arch that calls to everyone to make the same choice I did. Even if I am healed but for an instant, since the mind of God's Son is one—"When I am healed I am not healed alone" (W-pI.137)—my healed mind becomes the light that shines in the darkness of the world, inviting all to nestle within this sacred arch of peace. It is not something I do; the love with which I identify is the invitation—the natural effect of the mind's healing. Needless to say, we are not speaking of a collection of bodies underneath the arch, but rather the mind. Therefore, we practice in the very specific relationships that are our lives' classrooms. And as we accept the light within, it shines throughout the one mind of the Sonship.

In this context, two wonderful lines from Walt Whitman's "Song of Myself"* come to mind:

---

* "Whoever Degrades Another Degrades Me" was the title of an Academy class, held at the Foundation in July 2005.

> Whoever degrades another degrades me, and whatever is done or said returns at last to me. By God, I will accept nothing which all cannot have their counterpart of on the same terms.

The second line especially expresses the heart of life under the arch of forgiveness: If you judge one person, you must be ready to apply that same judgment to everyone. We are one, and our thoughts of one are thoughts of all. The well-known scriptural verse makes the same point, where Jesus says: "What you do to the least of these my children you do unto me" (Matthew 25:40). This applies to everyone, so that whenever we judge someone, we must be willing to make the same judgment of Jesus, not to mention everyone else. Therefore, when you seek to crucify, humiliate, or degrade another, you must be willing to make the same comments about Jesus or any other ego-free person.*

On the other hand, if you think of Jesus as total love and innocence, in whom shines the resplendence of Christ's light, you must be willing to share the same thought with those who seem to embody the ego's evil, darkness, and sin. If the light of Christ does not shine in all, it shines in none. Once again, the reality that is God's one Son means that if you separate from

---

* This discussion is continued in Chapter 5.

others through judgment and attack, you deny the oneness of God's Son, re-enacting the ontological instant when we separated from God and told Him His Son was now a thing apart.

Whitman's "Whoever degrades another degrades me" provides another aspect to our usual discussions of attacking others through judgment, or ourselves through sickness. Rarely, if ever, do we think that if one person attacks another, it is also an attack on us. As an example, consider the contemporary political scene in this country—the right- and left-wing divisions. There are many right-wing talk show hosts who revel in humiliating and degrading people on the left. If you happen to be of the same political persuasion and enjoy listening to attacks on those you see as enemies, you are attacking the whole Sonship. Similarly, if you are on the left and enjoy people degrading and making fun of President Bush, you but do the same thing. It does not matter which side you are on. When you enjoy listening to someone attacking another whom you do not like, it is the same as if you attacked that person yourself, and thus you will not escape the hellish consequences of your guilt, as we read in *The Song of Prayer*:

> Hell cannot be asked for another, and escaped by him who asks for it. Only those who are in hell can ask for hell (S-1.III.2:5-6).

The only true fact in the illusion is that we are the same. This is not the oneness of Heaven's undifferentiated spirit, which is unknown here. Yet while here, we *can* experience that truth's reflection in recognizing that we are one in having the same split mind: the wrong-minded ego, the right-minded Holy Spirit, and the power to choose between them. Bodies, on the other hand, are different. When we seek to degrade or humiliate someone—seeing our sins in them—we deny this inherent sameness. For example, Michael Moore's *Fahrenheit 911* is a funny and clever movie. Yet a good part of the movie's humor comes at President Bush's expense. It is one thing to disagree with someone's policies, yet quite another to mock the person. Unfortunately, that was one source of the movie's popularity, certainly among the left. In truth, however, it degraded one who is part of the Sonship, in whom the light of Christ shines just as it does in you, me, and Jesus. To say it is not present in this one person because you disagree with his policies, or think his I.Q. is not as high as a president's should be, is to attack the entire Sonship. It is the universality of forgiveness that makes the practice of this course so very difficult. Making fun of someone—a not-so-subtle form of judgment—is never justified. You cannot judge without attack and without a prior belief we are separate from each other.

On the other hand, there is a scene in Moore's movie that does not degrade anyone, though it makes a powerful statement regarding Congress passing the Patriot Act without reading it. In terms of its implications, this is a most significant bill. Congress passed it in the middle of the night, even though there was no way its members could have read it, given its size of 711 pages. Not even the staff that normally reads the bills and advises the Congressional membership would have had time to read it. In the movie, Moore rents an ice-cream truck with a speaker system and drives around Washington, in effect saying: "I am really trying to be helpful, guys. I know you didn't have a chance to read the bill, so here is what it says." Then he reads parts of it. He was not humiliating or attacking anyone, because he was not being personal, and his clever point was unmistakable. Similarly, Moore could have made his points about Bush without mocking him. Such motivation in making this movie is hardly kind and loving.

It is certainly important in a democracy that people express their concerns over what they believe is happening politically. Yet it is just as important that they be aware there are large groups of people who believe that what is going on is good. Similarly, many think *A Course in Miracles* is the work of the devil or the ego. We therefore need a perception that sees that all parties in a disagreement are one. Again, if George Bush is not part of the Sonship, if he is not weeping bitterly inside as is everyone else, no one is. By humiliating someone, whether a family member, boss, co-worker, or public official, we say that the Sonship is what the ego always maintained: a place of separation, judgment, and differences, and therefore a place of guilt. Above all it is the home of good guys and bad guys, of winners and losers, of those to be saved and those to be damned. We can therefore speak of two arches: the ego's arch of illusion and judgment, and Jesus' arch of reflected truth and forgiveness, to which we now turn.

3. The Two Arches:
The Ego's Body and Jesus' Love

The wrong mind and body are the ego's arch, and the right mind is Jesus' arch. The ego tells us the body will keep us safe, but the truth is that only love provides the safety for which we long. This is the context for our brief look at the opening and closing paragraphs of "What Is the Body?" from Part II of the workbook.

(W-pII.5.1:1-3) The body is a fence the Son of God imagines he has built, to separate parts of his Self from other parts. It is within this fence he thinks he lives, to die as it decays and crumbles. For within this fence he thinks that he is safe from love.

This is an important statement that reveals the ego's purpose in making the body, and in a larger sense, in making the world: they keep us safe from love. Because love is in the mind, it is crucial that we not see Jesus as a body. He is the Western world's greatest symbol of love, and if we insist on bringing him into the world and the body where he is not, we will never know him. We will know an image we have made, but we will not know *him*, and therefore will not know his love. However, what we *will* know, since we are talking about the body, is special love.

(1:4-5) Identifying with his safety [his body]**, he regards himself as what his safety is. How else could he be certain he remains within the body, keeping love outside?**

It is not only that we live within a body, we *are* the body. We put on a costume and then never take it off. After a while, it becomes grafted onto our skin and becomes our self. It is not only a defense; it becomes our identity. We thus have to realize that our entire life is dedicated to this body, which is why we need to expend a great deal of effort, especially at first, to fight the ego's heavy overlearning.

"Identifying with his safety, he regards himself as what his safety is." On the one hand, we believe the body is our safety; on the other hand, since we believe the body can hurt us, we need other bodies to protect us from those that will bring our bodies harm. Consequently, our entire day is geared toward taking care of the body. This is self-evident. Even when we study *A Course in Miracles* or some other spiritual teaching, we are concerned with the body—our physical, psychological self. We want a happier or redeemed self, but this is our bodily identity. This explains why people try to compromise the Course by relating to it as a physical, etheric, astral, or spiritual body; yet they remain *individual bodies*, differentiating one person from another. Again, it takes hard work to maintain and preserve the body; and many spiritual disciplines are indeed difficult because they require the body's involvement in working at redemption and salvation. This course asks nothing of us except to look, which involves no effort, *unless we are resistant.*

Now to the closing paragraph, which picks up the content of the sentence we just read:

(5:1-2) You will identify with what you think will make you safe. Whatever it may be, you will believe that it is one with you.

Repeating our comments, if you feel you are safe under the ego's arch, you will be a body, because you will think the body protects you: being with another body makes you feel happy, loved, and safe; having one of the body's extensions called money provides you with security; having other bodies as extensions —children, for example—makes you feel fulfilled. It is always some aspect of the body you think will make you safe, and so you become that body. All this places you under the ego's arch, but there is an alternative you can choose:

(5:3-8) Your safety lies in truth, and not in lies. Love is your safety. Fear does not exist. Identify with love, and you are safe. Identify with love, and

you are home. Identify with love, and find your Self.

This is the arch of peace, where Jesus wants us to spend every day with him and his message. As we grow in his love, we find safety as we realize this is our home. Just as we had grafted the body onto ourselves and became this "rotting prison" (T-26.I.8:3), we now take love, not only as our safety, but as our identity. And thus we find our Self. At the very end, we become one with that love and Self, as we had first become one with the pillar of forgiveness. Keeping this or any comparable image in mind throughout the day allows us to see how quickly we move away from it. The ego will accuse us of betraying, abandoning, and rejecting love, while all that has truly happened is that we became afraid of it, and so stepped outside the arch.

Once outside the arch, therefore, I can never feel safe, always needing more and more and more: The love and attention you give me today will be gone tomorrow, and so you will have to give it to me again. I may get a high grade on a paper I wrote for you, which is fine, but I do not know if I will get an A on my next one, without which I will feel like a failure. I may make enough money today, but tomorrow I will need more. Nothing is ever enough, because happiness is not about money, high grades, or special love and attention; it is about choosing to live beneath Jesus' arch and outside the ego's bottomless pit of specialness.

Such indeed is the ego's world—a bottomless pit, because once God is excluded, nothing remains, compelling us always to seek to fill up the nothingness. Yet we fill it with nothing, and thus keep stealing nothing from the world, killing for it to fill up the nothingness inside. However, it is nothing filling up nothing, resulting in our having nothing. We do not want to look at this because we believe we are the nothingness that is the ego's arch. Thus we seek to cannibalize from others, convinced that if we are loved and someone gives us the attention we crave, we are not alone and are not nothing. The problem is that we steal from someone who is also nothing. That is why special relationships are so painful. There are the illusions of wonder, joy, happiness, and peace, but none of them lasts. The ego's arch has no foundation.

Therefore, whenever anything disrupts your peace, it is never for the reason you think. The *only* reason for your disquiet is that you stepped outside Jesus' arch and went to the ego's, to the wrong teacher in whom there is no safety. You will feel the terrible burden of responsibility because you are responsible for something that can never be worked out. You will always fail, because your needs can never be met in a truly satisfying and lasting way. You cannot meet the needs of others, because the body was made to be insatiable; for example, you fill your stomach one moment, and several hours later it has to be filled again; your lungs are filled, and 20 seconds later they have to be refilled; you are loved once, but it is not enough—you have to be loved again. *It is always something more*. That is how you know you are living under the wrong arch—the arch of lack and not the arch of peace, which is based only on abundance. Love is complete and whole, and is always there. You need not look for it, strive after it, or kill to get it. You simply accept it, and in your practice, see how quickly you move away from this simple task. Returning to what I said in the Introduction, as soon as you can in the morning, think about your day's purpose. In the "Rules for Decision" (T-30.I), Jesus asks us to think about the day we want—content, not form: a day of either peace or conflict, love or fear.

Lesson 261 reflects these same ideas:

> I will identify with what I think is refuge and security. I will behold myself where I perceive my strength, and think I live within the citadel where I am safe and cannot be attacked. Let me today seek not security in danger, nor attempt to find my peace in murderous attack. I live in God. In Him I find my refuge and my strength. In Him is my Identity.

> In Him is everlasting peace. And only there will I remember Who I really am (W-pII.261.1).

The *Who* is capitalized in the last sentence, giving us a clue as to the problem. If I leave God's refuge and security by stepping outside the arch, it is because I do not want to remember my Identity. If I know that staying within the pillars of peace means letting go of my grievances, specialness, and judgments, allowing me to remember Who I truly am as God's Son, and I remain angry, judgmental, and disquieted, it must be that I am resisting attainment of the goal. If giving up judgment is the way to remember my Self, and I retain my anger, it must be that I do not want to remember my Identity. The text repeatedly explains that we cling to our judgments because in the presence of the Self, the *I* with which I identify does not exist. Acknowledging this fear allows me to be honest with myself and say: "If I am not at peace, it is not because of what you have or have not done, or anything external, but because I became afraid of the peace of God."

Q: I become terribly fearful when someone is angry and yells at me. Does that reflect my unconscious fear of God—that this person's wrath is nothing compared to how mad God is at me?

A: Yes, but you would not be upset by someone's anger with you if you did not unconsciously believe the person were justified, even if that person were having a psychotic episode and the anger had nothing to do with you. Everyone is having psychotic episodes all the time anyway, but the attack would have no effect unless you first believed it were due you. That is the problem. The only reason you believe God is angry is that you believe you deserve His wrath. It is a given that behind everyone you are afraid of or upset with is God. In working with this fact, however, it is important to realize, again, that you could not be upset unless you believed you deserved punishment. If that self-image were not there, it would not matter what anyone did or said. As unloving and unkind as another may be, you could not be affected unless you believed attack against yourself were justified.

Q: I was thinking about the ego's alliance with the body and how someone yelling at me, even a baby crying, triggers a physiological reaction—an adrenaline rush, for example. When that happens, I find it almost impossible to be clear in my mind.

A: That is the purpose of the emotional trigger. The purpose of a physiology that pumps adrenaline is to convince us we are bodies. *Purpose* is emphasized throughout *A Course in Miracles*, for it unifies our perceptions, reflecting the ego's single purpose behind everything and calling to mind Polonius' words about Hamlet: "Though this be madness, yet there is method in it." Even though the ego is insane, there is a method or purpose in its use of the body: to convince us we are mindless creatures. Thus we can justifiably say we cannot help what we are feeling. For example, if someone threatens us physically, the body's manufacture of adrenaline is inevitable as long as we identify with the physical. When, however, we realize we are a mind, and the body is simply its projection, we understand that the body can serve either the ego's purpose of fear, or the Holy Spirit's purpose of teaching us peace. It is our choice, and when we choose peace, nothing external can affect us.

The body is a compelling witness for its own reality —"propaganda for itself" (T-27.IV.5:3)—as well as the reality of the thought system that made it. That is why it was made, and made a certain way. Just as our dreams at night take shape from our thoughts, so does the body arise both from our belief we are separate and our intent on protecting the separation by sealing it within the mind's vault, pretending that what is within the mind is now in an autonomous and self-directed body. As our physiology changes over time, our lives seem to change as well. We say we go through puberty, adolescence, and other physiological sus' Love

ompanied by hormonal changes that ions and behavior. However, those the cause of our bodily fixations or ch come rather from the mind's deci- sio ts self-concept be displaced onto the body, leaving us perpetually at the mercy of laws and forces beyond our control.

It is difficult when in the midst of an intense body reaction to step back and say this is the mind's dream. Being fearful of a hurricane about to strike your home is a legitimate thing for a body to feel, so try to refrain from analyzing it or giving a metaphysical interpretation to your reaction. At some point, however, try to be aware that the intensity of your fear and anxiety is not coming from the fact that your house is on the verge of being destroyed, or your family about to be hurt. The real impetus for these bodily concerns and feelings does not come from the external situation. Do not deny what your body is feeling—that is the worst thing you can do, and this course certainly does not advocate such denial. Yet when you have climbed high on the ladder, you can be in the midst of a bodily-traumatic situation—for you or others—and remain peaceful. Whatever your body might do, it would be as if you were merely watching it, for you would know you are not your body, nor are others theirs.

However, do not pretend you are at that stage when the body is still a major concern for you. *A Course in*

Miracles is for people on the bottom of the ladder. While it comes from the highest source imaginable, it is directed at the lowest level because it meets us where we think we are—the body with its specific needs. The bottom of the ladder is thus about bodily concerns, where we deal with specifics and demand that God, the Holy Spirit, Jesus, and this course meet these needs. Jesus does not say this is bad or that we should avoid doing that. He simply cautions us by saying this is only the beginning of the journey; not the middle, and certainly not the end. We will not get to the end, however, unless we start at the beginning, which means our bodily preoccupations—ours and others'. We therefore start with the body, but will certainly not end up there.

This is why it takes quite a while before students of *A Course in Miracles* begin to understand it is not written for them as a body, even though the language suggests it is, with God Himself depicted in bodily terms. The ego is referred to with the pronoun *it*, but not the Holy Spirit, Who is a *He*. God, too, is presented as a Person, as, of course, is Jesus. Why? Because we think *we* are persons. We therefore need to accept this perceptual fact and not skip over the steps of our experience, but we also do not want to make perception a reality. The Course is written on many different levels, and as we progress on our journey up the ladder, each rung, in a sense, takes us deeper into understanding what the Course is saying. That is why students have the experience of reading a sentence they know they have seen before, but now understand it, or they read a sentence they swear they never saw earlier. What is impressive about the Course as a pedagogical technique, as well as a spirituality, is that it is written in such a way that no matter where we are on the ladder, we will benefit from it.

The problem students get into is wanting to remain on the bottom rung. Thus they keep insisting this course is about living life better as a body within the dream. They insist the Course is written for them as a person; that the Holy Spirit is a Person; and that the personal God hears their prayers—with ears, obviously. You will never grow if you remain at this level of perception. I have often said in workshops that a wonderful way to begin the journey with Jesus is to relate to him as an older brother. However, if you see him only as one who is always there for you, you will forever be a small child and will not grow. Helen's lovely poem "A Jesus Prayer" begins with: "A Child, a Man and then a Spirit" (*The Gifts of God*, p. 82). The point of our prayer is that we would grow up to become like Jesus. We begin as a child, develop into adulthood, and end as a spirit, the poem's symbol for being in the real world. And so the idea is to use *A Course in Miracles* where we believe we are, but to keep the mind open so we can be led more deeply into its thought system and grow from childhood to spiritual adulthood. Our next chapter will consider the symbols of the child and its song.

4. The Child's Song

The idea of a child can be approached in two ways. In *A Course in Miracles*, being a child is essentially negative. A child throws temper tantrums and demands that its needs be met when it wants them met, with no concern for anyone else. Jesus uses the phrase "little wisdom of a child" (T-29.IX.6:4), for the child does not understand the language of adults, and insists that what it sees and feels is reality. Thus children play make-believe, having an ability to project onto their toys and make them real; this is no different, however, from what we as adults do with the illusory world. We play with different toys, but the content is the same, for we, too, think our toys mean something—whether we are shooting guns in war, making business deals, or seeking to dispose of people we do not like.

This is the war of specialness, where you and I meet on the battleground to see who can kill the other first, and gain as much as possible from the victory. In special love, we try to cannibalize each other, without having it look as if that is what we are doing. We sit down, as it were, at the ego's bargaining table: I need something from you to make up for a lack in me, but I know you are not going to supply it because you took it from me in the first place. Since you are not going to return it, I have to pay for it, which I bitterly resent. The bargain is that I will pay you for what I want from you; and naturally I will give as little as possible, which is *me*. I attempt to discern what you need, and of course you do the very same thing with me. This is how relationships function in the world, the game of specialness that children play when they are outside the arch.*

Yet there is another child, described in Lesson 182. This is the Child within that appears little because our fear is so great. Jesus asks us to nourish this Child, thinking of It as what we grow into, which living beneath the arch brings about. We need to remember that the arch represents the framework within which we want to live our day, and think of as often as we can. We ask Jesus to remind us of our safety when we are with him, for outside his arch of peace we are vulnerable, which means any time we feel vulnerable to a hurricane, abusive relationship, depressed stock market, uncaring president or prime minister, it is always because we are outside the arch, living as a spoiled child that revels in being miserable so it can blame everyone around it. That is why we made ourselves

---

* See, e.g., "The Choice for Completion" (T-16.V); "The Treachery of Specialness" (T-24.II); and my discussion in *The Message of A Course in Miracles,* Vol. One, pp. 150-57.

with a healthy pair of lungs: so we could cry and scream, making people pay attention to us.

The Two Songs

The songs we hear outside this arch are those of battle—the discordant, dissonant sounds of the ego's world, where nothing and no one is in harmony with anyone else. People sing their songs in their own key, their voices themselves being off pitch—dissonant with everyone else's song, because few care about blending into one sound, as in a great chorus. We almost all want *our* sound and song. This is the "dirge" Jesus speaks of in the *Psychotherapy* pamphlet when he says that healing begins "when the patient begins to hear the dirge he sings, and questions its validity" (P-2.VI.1:5). It is the song we sing to ourselves, believing ours to be the only song in the universe. If it does not sound right, we are certain it is because others are out of tune, not us. You can imagine the cacophony that results when everyone thinks his or hers is the only song. Yet this is our world: a cacophonous mass of raucously ugly sounds. We live with these shrieks of the ego and train ourselves to hear only our song, uninterested in anyone else's.

Whenever you feel such dissonance, know it has nothing to do with the bad guys "out there." Under the arch, the song you hear and sing—the song you are—blends with everyone else's, and there is no disharmony, as in the lovely phrase from the Course wherein we all "join the mighty chorus to the Love of God" (T-26.IV.6:3). The actual notes might differ, but they blend together and in the end become one note. In the passage from *The Rainbow*, little Anna grows to adulthood within the arch of her parents, in turn developing an arch with her partner.

Reflected in this discussion is the idea of shared versus separate interests. When we step outside the arch, our interests are separate, and, again, we think only of our own music, with no concern for listening to anyone else. Within the arch, however, we are a child wanting Jesus to be our older brother, next to whom we grow strong, eventually becoming like him and a pillar for others. Yet we cannot grow unless we first accept our childhood state and learn from Jesus that everyone is truly under the arch with us, singing the same song. To be sure, there are different harmonies and voice intonations. Yet it is the same song because we share the same interest to grow together. At the end, even this song disappears, along with the arch, leaving God's Love as the only reality.

It is important to use this concept—in this or any other meaningful image—to frame your day. By so doing, it will not matter if a hurricane destroys your home, or a medical condition threatens your family or yourself. Under this arch of peace and safety you will recognize all situations—positive or negative—as simply part of the chorus, and the sounds will be sweet whether or not the weather forecast is ominous for you or your home, or whether the doctor gives you good or bad news. The song will sound just as beautiful, and you need to ask yourself: "Is this what I want, or do I want the dissonance that is my life?" This is the choice, and you *do* have a choice. You cannot choose most external events, but you can choose how you will see them—from within the arch or outside it. Therefore, the questions are which teacher do you want and under which principle will you live your life—shared or separate interests? Nothing matters but that decision, for it is the choice for Heaven or hell.

The deep sin of which each of us accuses ourselves is selfishness. It is not really the sin of murdering God; besides, no one has a clue as to what that really means. Yet we all know what it means to be selfish. The ultimate selfishness is indeed reflected in what we did with our Creator, for we did not care about Him, His Love, or His Son, caring only for ourselves. We thus live selfish lives here, lodging our guilt even more deeply. Once we step outside the arch, we are back into the self-centered life of *me, myself, and I.* All that is important is *me*, or those with whom I identify—family, friends, a group, or a cause. Within the arch, on the other hand, we recognize that our goal is, in fact, to be selfish, meaning Self-ish, because within that Self we recognize our inherent unity as God's one Son.

Q: As I was checking out of the motel this morning, the clerk was on the phone taking a reservation. Standing there I thought: "I am here in person and should be taken care of first! Why are you talking to this person on the phone?" I was struck by the fact that I really meant it. I also realized that if I were the one on the phone, I would be thinking that I was the most important person and should be attended to before anyone else.

A: That kind of experience is helpful. It is a minor, circumscribed event, but behind it lies a chasm of selfishness that is in everyone. It is helpful to see it in relatively trivial things, for it tends to be easier to see the problem more clearly, but if it is there in one instance, it is always there. We all have split minds—a right and wrong mind, but we cannot get to the right mind without first looking at the wrong mind.

Q: If we are not having experiences of the timeless as we deal with this seemingly bottomless chasm of selfishness and self-hatred, wouldn't it still be helpful to at least intellectually understand that the self we are so bound to is not the real Self, and that there is a Self that replaces the self of the dualistic world? If we stick with that, eventually glimpses of that Self will come through—isn't that correct?

A: Yes, absolutely. There are lovely passages that describe how we get glimpses of the lilies behind the veil (T-20.I.4; T-20.II.9). One of the advantages of using the ladder as a symbol is that it allows us to talk about the process from beginning to End, at the same time respecting where we are on the ladder. The top is the real world, and once there, everything disappears, including the ladder itself, and we are back with God and our Self. Before that final step, however, we are aware of the goal and the journey to get there, and staying beneath the arch helps us maintain that awareness. This is the shift in perspective that is Jesus' goal for us, and so it is certainly helpful to know where we are heading, and that we make our way slowly since fear still accompanies us.

"The Forgiving Dream"

We look now at the part of "The Forgiving Dream" (T-29.IX) that discusses childhood, beginning with the ego, and then moving to the real world.

The Ego's Child

The next paragraph begins with a line borrowed from St. Paul:

(6:1) There is a time when childhood should be passed and gone forever.

Jesus tells us in many different ways in the Course that at some point we have to grow up. He is not speaking of childhood as a developmental stage of life, but as an *attitude*—the self-centered neediness typical of a child.

(6:2-3) Seek not to retain the toys of children. Put them all away, for you have need of them no more.

If you no longer have need of childhood toys, it is because you no longer see your body as primary. Since the body's demands keep us as children, spiritual maturity according to *A Course in Miracles* comes from moving from identification with the body to the mind—from mindlessness to mindfulness. The child wants only that its needs be met. It cannot live on its own and is totally dependent on others. Consequently, it learns quite early about special love bargains. If it is cute and sweet, a good little boy or girl, its needs will be met more quickly and more frequently. It also learns how to play special hate: to punish, withhold love, and make things difficult for its parents, who it thinks have made things so difficult for it.

Special relationships are focused on the body, for that is where specialness is acted out, even though its home rests in the mind's decision to join with the ego instead of the Holy Spirit. We project the special relationship from the mind, where we have identified with the ego's thought of sin, and this leads us to identify with the sinful body—except its sinfulness is now someone else's fault. These relationships are the children's games we play, and as long as we identify with the body and our needs, we require the ego's special toys. As we begin to live under the arch, however, our need for these toys falls away, because our only need now is to learn forgiveness—the principle of shared rather than separate interests. *One or the other* is no longer attractive to us, for it does not lead us home, but *together, or not at all* most assuredly does. To see that we all share the same insanity and sanity is the perception that helps us grow.

Jesus now becomes more specific, as we move to judgment, one of the major themes of this section:

(6:4-6) The dream of judgment is a children's game, in which the child becomes the father, powerful, but with the little wisdom of a child. What hurts him is destroyed; what helps him, blessed. Except he judges this as does a child, who does not know what hurts and what will heal.

A perfect description of special love and special hate: if you give me what I want, I will love you; if you do not, I will punish you. Infants and children are experts at this dynamic, as we all know. But adults are as well: we reward our friends and punish our enemies in the same way. Indeed, all groups act like this, and so the laws of specialness apply to individuals, families, businesses, nation states, and religious, racial, and economic groups. Only those who give us what we want are our friends; the rest, our enemies.

This, then, sums up the section, and every other section as well. The dream of judgment is of being separated—individual, special, and selfish—as we now make judgments with "the little wisdom of a child": what hurts us is bad; what helps is good. Except, how do we know what truly hurts or helps us? What we think helps is whatever reinforces our bodily identity as a separate and innocent self; what hurts is whatever challenges that self-concept. And so, whenever we divide the world into what is good and what is bad, we know we are being a little child living outside the arch. Yet, those judgments are how we all live. Is it good for us, or is it bad? Growing up in a Jewish home, one of the recurring phrases I heard was: "Is it good for the Jews?" A president makes a decision: is it good for the Jews? We invade Korea: is it good for the Jews? I was with Helen in her home when John Hinckley made an attempt on President Reagan's life, and the very first question from her Guyanese housekeeper was: "Was he black?" If he were, that would obviously have been bad for the blacks.

This is the way we think as individuals and as members of groups. Is this good for me or bad? The hurricane is bad for me; therefore, I do not like it. But there are people for whom the hurricane is good. If you own a hardware store, for example, the hurricane is good for business. Whatever is judged as good for one, is bad for another, and vice versa. Almost everyone would agree that war is bad, except for the arms merchants who make out like bandits. My brother is a securities analyst, and I remember that before the first Gulf war he recommended that his firm buy stock in Raytheon, the company that made the weapons and bombs for that war; so his firm made a lot of money. Raytheon was thus good for him, but bad for the Iraqis.

This, then, is another way of looking at selfishness: whatever helps we bless; whatever hurts we punish. We all live this life of the child, yet under the arch everything is seen differently. If something hurts even one person, it is bad—not in a sinful sense, certainly, but bad because it is the ego's judgment that excludes, attacks, and therefore maintains our identity as children. If something helps everyone, it is good, and there is only one thing that fits that category—forgiveness, the principle that facilitates our growth under the arch. Our practice, therefore, should involve observing specifically how our days reflect this principle that good is what helps us and bad is what hurts us. Because we are little children, we do not recognize that thoughts of guilt and attack hurt us and therefore must hurt everyone. The truth, however, is that what helps us (forgiveness and healing) helps everyone.

Your day, thus, should be geared toward keeping yourself under the arch of peace as much as possible, where everyone is welcome without exception. See, then, how quickly you step outside, and you will know you have done so when you feel twinges of anxiety, annoyance, anger, or even feelings of excitement. At that point, tell yourself you became frightened of the love that excludes no one and includes everyone, and so you once again left Jesus and his arch.

(6:7) And bad things seem to happen, and he is afraid of all the chaos in a world he thinks is governed by the laws he made.

This is not conscious, but what we made to govern our world are laws of scarcity, loss, and deprivation. Bad things happen and they happen to us personally, yet we never want to recognize how happy we are when they do. Behind anxiety and the fear of the coming hurricane, for example, is the secret joy that, once again, we are innocent victims—it is not our fault! Even as our bodies are in agony, psychologically and physically, there is part of us that revels in the pain, because it affirms once again that we are off the hook. Within our delusional system, moreover, we have no memory that it is our dream and that we want calamities to befall us. The ego's bottom line remains: I exist, but I am not responsible.

Now the other side:

The Real World

(6:8-9) Yet is the real world unaffected by the world he thinks is real. Nor have its laws been changed because he does not understand.

The fact that we do not understand the laws of the arch does not mean we are not living under it. Moreover, when under the arch, we are unaffected by the world: "Yet is the real world unaffected by the world he thinks is real." The real world is the state of mind that is free from sin, judgment, and attack; it is the world we gradually move into under the arch. Once again, our daily practice of forgiveness helps the Child in us to grow. Needless to say, the Christ does not grow—*our awareness of Christ grows*, and thus the image of a little Child that grows over time.

If I find myself affected by something external, I know I am living in the ego's world, not Jesus'. My only question then becomes: why would I continually choose to live in a world that is so painful and brings so much hurt, when I could as easily be back with Jesus under his arch where no one loses, no one hurts, and we all grow to remember our Self? We need to pose this question every moment of the day, and try as quickly as we can to move from the experience of disquiet—whatever its form—to its cause, which is the fear of the love and innocence beneath the arch. This fear impelled us to step back into the world of hate, guilt, and separation, and we simply need to know this is what we have done. Applying that principle as often as we can during the day helps us finally to choose again, to say and mean: I do not want to do this any more.

(7:1-4) The real world still is but a dream. Except the figures have been changed. They are not seen as idols which betray. It is a dream in which no one is used to substitute for something else, nor interposed between the thoughts the mind conceives and what it sees.

The real world is an illusion because it is not Heaven, but it is also not part of the ego's dream. Nothing exists in the real world except the reflection of Heaven's Oneness, and we know this world is a dream. There is nobody—*no body*—to interfere with remembering our Self, for everything is seen as mind, and people seen as sharing one interest and goal. In other words, no one is used to substitute for God's Love, because we recognize Its reflection in all people, with no one excluded.

Our purpose, therefore, is to begin as a child and grow, ultimately attaining the real world. This is the final state of life under the arch, the consummation of the choice to be under it, with Jesus as one pillar and forgiveness the other. Until that final consummation, we step in and out. Seeing another's interests as separate from our own places us outside, where we care only about ourselves and the satisfaction of our needs; we no longer hear the melody of love and oneness, but the dissonance of the ego's songs of guilt and judgment. Back within, however, we still hear those other sounds—we know there are disasters in the world; for example, brutal wars and ravaging famines, or the hurricane that destroyed our home. Yet we do not give these dissonances power to disrupt or destroy our song; we no longer allow what people do to affect the reality of Jesus' song of oneness, because we recognize that people's hurtful expressions of hate and cruelty mask their sweet sounds of love. These fear-driven people are under that arch with us, but do not realize it. We see the special love and hate relationships that keep people separated, and which they use to aggrandize their little selves at another's expense, but we also recognize that their fear, anger, and cruelty come from the vulnerability that inevitably follows separation from the arch of love and peace. With this recognition, the love with which we identify calls to them through us, inviting them to make the same choice we made and to come home. It is therefore not that we do not see and hear what goes on in the world, but that we see and hear differently—coming from a perspective of love rather than separation and hate.

In summary, life under Jesus' arch hears the disharmonies in the world but gives them no power over the lovely song we know we are. Our love, which strengthens as we draw ever closer to the pillar we call Jesus, calls to everyone to come to where we are, with him. We understand, with compassion, that all who think they are not there are in great pain. That is all we truly hear. When we hear the pain, we touch it gently and sing Jesus' comforting song, which soothes all suffering. If, on the other hand, what we hear is hate, meanness, and selfishness, we will not touch them. Yet, if we translate meanness into the pain of being outside the arch, our hearts will go out to embrace it, and sounds of love will flow through us and call people to return. And so our day should be about hearing the song of pain under the dirge of cruelty, for we want to hear it in ourselves. However, if we do not allow love to extend *through* us to embrace others, we will not let it extend *in* us. We would thus separate from love, placing us once again outside the arch.

(7:5-6) No one is used for something he is not, for childish things have all been put away. And what was once a dream of judgment now has changed into a dream where all is joy, because that is the purpose that it has.

Remember, "childish things" are defined here as thoughts of judgment and specialness. In the "dream of judgment," everyone is seen as separate, and the only criterion for evaluating something as good is whether it is good for *me*—not good for *all*. When this purpose has been shifted to seeing shared interests, the result is true joy. Indeed, what could be more joyful than to know we are home—safe, secure, and loved? Every child wants this; we all want this. As we begin to hear love's song of safety, we need to ask why we would ever choose to give that up. We should ask that question whenever peace has disappeared, its place taken by guilt, anger, depression, and fear. After all, who in their right minds would choose not to be in this place of security, safety, and love?

(7:7-8) Only forgiving dreams can enter here, for time is almost over. And the forms that enter in the dream are now perceived as brothers, not in judgment, but in love.

You begin to realize that everyone you invite is a part of you, just as you are part of love, and love is part of you. Then watch the fear of love begin to rise. Your fear of its perfect oneness causes you to push people away and give them power over you. Thus you allow even the most trivial things to upset you—e.g., the way a person eats, walks, or smiles—forgetting that what is upsetting is not what your eyes see, but that you believe you abandoned love and will never find it again; and even if you did, the arch would be forever barred to you. This is the source of your pain, and what you try to project onto others.

(8:1-2) Forgiving dreams have little need to last. They are not made to separate the mind from what it thinks.

Dreams of judgment separate the mind from its guilt, making a world and body onto which the repressed guilt can be projected. In forgiving dreams, however, everything is accepted. We had first accepted guilt and fear as true, coming from the belief that we betrayed love. We then moved beyond the sin to the love, which means love was not abandoned, betrayed, or destroyed—nothing happened and nothing changed. Accepting the darkness of our thoughts allowed us to accept the light of the real thought, and in that light recognize that everyone is there with us. Indeed, it is impossible that anyone not be there.

(8:3) They do not seek to prove the dream is being dreamed by someone else.

This is a major theme in *A Course in Miracles*: scarcity becomes deprivation, wherein my life of lack, ineptitude, and inferiority—I am missing what everyone else seems to have—is a result of what was done to me. Whether it was my upbringing, genes, past lifetimes, or God, someone did this to me and made me what I am. We seek always to prove that another dreams our dreams and is the cause of our unhappiness and distress. Once we fall into this scarcity-deprivation trap, we know for certain we are outside the arch.

(8:4) And in these [forgiving] **dreams a melody is heard that everyone remembers, though he has not heard it since before all time began.**

This is the melody Jesus speaks of in "The Forgotten Song" (T-21.I) and *The Song of Prayer* (S-1.I)—what the Holy Spirit sings to us. This melody has but a single note—love, the one note of God's one Son. As long as we think we are here in a body, we will not hear this melody of the Mind, but only its reflection. In the world, we hear different voices and different parts of the melody, but under the arch they blend into one. We should not deny the separate voices; rather, we need to hear harmony where before we heard discordant notes and clashing melodies. Within the pillars of forgiveness, the dissonant sounds become one, joined in beautiful harmony that recalls "the mighty chorus to the Love of God" (T-26.IV.6:3). As the text ends, Jesus reflects his final vision:

> And as each one elects to join with me [Jesus], the song of thanks from earth to Heaven grows from tiny scattered threads of melody to one inclusive chorus from a world redeemed from hell, and giving thanks to You (T-31.VIII.11:5).

This, then, is what we hear under the arch. We recognize differences, but understand that these differences make no difference because they sound so beautiful together—conflict is gone, since despite different forms, the content is one. Only outside the arch does everything conflict with everything else. This is inevitable, but not because of what is outside. Conflict develops only when we *think* we are outside the arch. In truth, there is nothing outside at all—no world, no separate bodies—only an insane thought system teaching us that there is. Within the arch, however, all these illusions disappear.

This understanding moves us from abstract principles to specific guidelines for living on a practical basis, day in and day out. Everyone and everything is seen as serving the same purpose, and as you become aware of seeing another as different from you, affecting your well being, you know you stepped outside the arch by deciding you no longer want Jesus as your teacher or forgiveness as your guiding principle. Instead, you chose the ego's principle of judgment—*one or the other*. That is why you are never upset for the reason you think (W-pI.5). The cause of your distress is never outside; you are upset only because you decided to step out from under this loving arch.

Again, this is the question we need to ask ourselves: "What is wrong with me that I would leave such love and safety?" It is the same question we should have asked at the beginning, when we seemed to leave Heaven as one. We did not ask it then, but we can ask it now. Note that the question is not what is wrong with *you*, but what is wrong with *me* that I would choose to leave this arch of peace? Once we hear the Holy Spirit's melody, it becomes increasingly difficult to justify not hearing it—its soft and gentle sweetness is so compelling we could never again totally believe in the ego. As soon as we become anxious, angry, depressed, or excited, we need try to think of this melody, and its remembrance will call us back to sanity.

There is a wonderful scene in Mozart's *Die Zauberflöte* (*The Magic Flute*) where the hero Tamino plays his flute and the wild animals become docile.

We all possess that flute and can play Tamino's lovely melody—the instrument we hear under the arch, playing the melody of forgiveness that silences the ego's raucous shrieks, the "thunder of the meaningless" (W-pI.106.2:1). Other bodies might not necessarily change, but in our minds the roaring lion cuddles next to us, and the raging tiger becomes a playful kitten. When we play the *miracle* flute and hear the sweet melody that makes no one different or separate, guilt disappears. Without guilt there is nothing to fear, since fear only follows from projected guilt. That is why in the early weeks of the scribing, when Helen complained to Jesus about her fears and asked him to take them away he replied, to paraphrase, "I cannot take your fear away because I did not make it; but I can help you undo its cause: the willingness to be separate" (see T-2.VI.4). Jesus was succinctly presenting to Helen the message of his course: "I will help you in your mind, not in the world. I cannot change your dream, for I am not dreaming it; but I can help you undo the fear that is the dream's origin. Moreover, your fear comes from choosing to be separate from me—stepping outside my arch. If you are fearful, anxious, angry, or impatient, it is only because you left my love. Stay close to me, and you, too, will become this pillar of peace."

That is what Jesus tells us all: "I cannot help you outside the arch. I know there is no 'outside the arch,' but I can remind you so you will know it, too. You but make all this up. Your raging lions and tigers of attack are the mere projections of your guilt." Every time we become disquieted, therefore, Jesus will hand us his miracle flute of forgiveness to play, if we let him, and everything will change because we will be listening to his melody of love. In its presence, nothing can hurt us, and so when we are threatened by anyone or anything, it is simply because we put the flute down once again.

(8:5) Forgiveness, once complete, brings timelessness so close the song of Heaven can be heard, not with the ears, but with the holiness that never left the altar that abides forever deep within the Son of God.

We do not hear Heaven's song with ears—just as vision is not perceived through eyes—but with the holiness that never left the altar, which is the mind's decision maker. Jesus refers to the altar that comes to symbolize our choice for the Holy Spirit instead of the ego. There are in fact two altars: one drips with blood when we choose the ego's murderous world; the other is strewn with lilies of forgiveness, which opens to the altar of love that abides forever deep within the heart of God's Son.

(8:6) And when he hears this song again, he knows he never heard it not.

When you hear even the faintest intimations of the song—experiencing shared rather than separate interests—you understand that your holding onto grievances, anxieties, and concerns is a defense against that song. Thus you can more quickly lay these problems aside. That is why the ego defends against it so heavily and why we identify so strongly with separation, judgment, and specialness. We are terrified, because we know on some level that if we let ourselves hear that melody and feel its love, we will no longer believe the ego, remembering there was never a time we did not hear that song. We then spend the remainder of our lives drawing closer to that melody within, not to recapture some past moment but to have it now, realizing it is only our dreams of judgment that keep us from it.

(8:7) And where is time, when dreams of judgment have been put away?

We live in a temporal world because it makes real the ego thought system of individuality. We commonly think we are the products of our past and must plan for the future; we hate and love in the present, based upon needs born of past experience, yet when judgment is gone, so is time. Under the arch of love, the laws of time and space disappear. There are no differences, for everyone is the same. Eyes may differentiate and perceive separation, but the mind realizes our inherent unity. Once again, we are part of the Sonship's glorious symphony, which has the illusion of separate parts, but in truth contains only one note and one instrument.

Jesus now encourages us to apply his lessons in our daily lives:

(9:1) Whenever you feel fear in any form,—and you *are* fearful if you do not feel a deep content, a certainty of help, a calm assurance Heaven goes with you,—be sure you made an idol, and believe it will betray you.

The words within the dashes reflect life under the arch: "a deep content, a certainty of help, a calm assurance Heaven goes with you." It is knowing that the love under the arch nourishes and protects you, as it did little Anna in Lawrence's novel. You need not pretend you are grown up; you merely allow the love and strength around you to grow, as you feel safe and comforted. If those feelings are absent, it means you merely stepped outside the arch, which impels you to seek special love and hate idols to keep the arch's rejected love hidden and buried.

It is helpful to understand that we leave the arch when we become fearful of the love that would negate our separated self. Yet we must increasingly recognize that living a life with idols of special love and hate—I love when you help me and meet my needs, and hate when you do not—does not make us happy. There is no "deep content," no "certainty of help," and no "calm assurance that Heaven goes with you" when you live in the world of specialness outside the arch.

(9:2) For beneath your hope that it [the idol of specialness] **will save you lie the guilt and pain of self-betrayal and uncertainty, so deep and bitter that the dream cannot conceal completely all your sense of doom.**

If we are truly honest, this is what we would recognize. Even when life seems to work—the world does our bidding by meeting our needs—somewhere inside we know the "good" will not last, and in the end God will exact His vengeance. That is when nightmarish attacks of anxiety appear out of nowhere and we develop one symptom after another—guilt is always projected. Freud was brilliant in describing how the mind's repressed guilt finds its means of expression, albeit in disguised forms. These horrible thoughts about ourselves thus make their way to the surface and invariably result in attack of one of two objects: the body of others or our own. When it is the former, we attack and judge them; when it is the latter, we become ill or indulge in self-sabotage. Yet all this has nothing to do with the body but with its source: the mind's decision to be separate.

Once the decision for the ego has been made, the totality of its thought system inevitably spins out. We are overwhelmed with guilt and believe God will punish and destroy us. Projecting this, we then believe that someone "out there" will punish and destroy us: the IRS, the boss, or this hated person. We walk around with a sense of doom—the Chicken Little mentality—wherein at some point the sky will come crashing down on us. Of course, in our guilt-ridden dream the sky does crash down in the end, for we all die. However, this is frequently couched in religious terms: e.g., God took this loved one back to Him; it was His doing. And indeed it was—the ego's god!

Underlying our dream of death is the guilt of our presumed Self-betrayal. *We* are the ones who crucified Christ, which explains the widespread popularity of the Christian myth—its source lies deep within everyone: all believe they are responsible for Christ's crucifixion, and, given the chance, would do it again and again; either as haters of Jesus or as followers who hate others in his name. Yet when we speak of the crucified Christ, we do not speak of Jesus. The Christ we dreamt we crucified is our Self. We project our sin, and then crucify others so we do not have to look at the fact that we are the crucifier *and* crucified. Recall this incisive line from the text: "The secret of salvation is but this: that you are doing this unto yourself" (T-27.VIII.10:1) *You* are not crucifying me; *I* am. I did not crucify Jesus; I crucified *me*. No one else can ever truly be responsible for crucifixion, or for being its victim.

(9:3) Your self-betrayal must result in fear, for fear *is* judgment, leading surely to the frantic search for idols and for death.

The subject here is guilt, which demands the punishment we fear. All this is based on judgment, we being the ultimate victim of our judgment. And so, in order to protect ourselves from the expected punishment from others, we make idols of specialness: love and hate—the world outside the arch. Again, when we return to Jesus' arch—the meaning of that lovely phrase, "turn you to the stately calm within." (T-18.I.8:2)—it is all different. That "stately calm" characterizes life under the arch—nothing can affect us, because there is nothing outside. Only our thoughts can harm us (see, e.g., W-pII.338), and when these thoughts of guilt, fear, and hate are brought to the love of Jesus under the arch, they simply dissolve, because they were nothing to begin with. Stepping out of that arch is *always* the problem, which leads us to define our needs—and the ego loves to define our needs, spiritual or otherwise. Yet there are no needs except to return to the arch, our home where we truly belong. In the opening of *The Song of Prayer*, Jesus tells us that in the experience of God's Love all needs are met, for they disappear into the truth (S-1.I.4). Our one need, therefore, is to remember we are loved, not by the world's special and exclusive love, but by a transmundane love that sees all God's Sons as one.

(10:1) Forgiving dreams remind you that you live in safety and have not attacked yourself.

This is the safety of life under love's arch. We have not attacked ourselves nor God, and so there is no sin, guilt, or fear. Indeed, fear is impossible without guilt: "The attraction of guilt produces fear of love" (T-19.IV-A.10:1). Our belief that we destroyed love is why we fear it. And we are afraid of forgiveness and releasing judgment because we are afraid of the love just behind our attack thoughts. That, ultimately, explains why we fear hurricanes, disasters, and loss of any kind: we believe love will exact its vengeance on us. We need only return to the arch, however, where we recognize there is no separation or guilt, and so nothing to fear.

(10:2) So do your childish terrors melt away, and dreams become a sign that you have made a new beginning, not another try to worship idols and to keep attack.

This is not the ego's new beginning, which is always the old beginning revisited, wherein we start again with another relationship—"another can be found" (W-pI.170.8:7)—wherein we dispense with one special partner and begin with another, hoping this time it will be different. Of course, probably two minutes into the relationship we know it is not going to be any different at all. We therefore pretend for two weeks, two months, two years, two decades, or two millennia. At some point, what we knew at the beginning is going to rear its ugly head, and then we will kill again and embark on still another beginning. Thus our lives: new beginnings that turn out to be old ones in disguise.

The new beginning of which Jesus speaks—leading into the opening section of Chapter 30—is our life under the arch. It is not an attempt to make a new beginning outside it by building a new house, getting a new partner, or starting a new business. There is a qualitative difference, for there is a new source, a new teacher, and a new home. Under the arch, therefore, our terrors melt away. They are childish terrors because they are made up, and illusions can have no real effect on us who live under Jesus' arch of safety.

(10:3) Forgiving dreams are kind to everyone who figures in the dream.

Note well the word *everyone*, and do not let its significance pass you by. The world's dream is one of separation, which becomes the dream of the real world when you bring everyone in through forgiveness. *Everyone*. A simple rule of thumb you can use to know when you have stepped outside the arch is that you do not see everyone as the same. *Whenever you see people as different, and the differences are important, you know you have stepped outside the arch.* Thus Jesus says his is a very simple course, for the sameness of God's Son is its only principle. When you are angry with others, or give them power to take away your peace, you make differences real. When you believe salvation rests in one particular person, or in one particular part of a person, or on one particular day or place, you know you have once more stepped beyond the arch.

Within the arch, again, there is no time or space and there are no separate bodies, though there remains a fleeting awareness of them. What is now in the forefront of awareness is our inherent sameness. It does not matter where we are, when, or whom we are with, the love under the arch is fully present, and everyone is part of its perfect peace. If a single person is excluded, love and peace are excluded. The peace of God that passes understanding, of which St. Paul wrote, is the peace that embraces everyone, without exception.

(10:4) And so they bring the dreamer full release from dreams of fear.

Our dreams of fear disappear when we realize that perception of differences and specialness needs are opportunities to correct our error and learn we are the same.

(10:5) He does not fear his judgment for he has judged no one...

The *his* in "does not fear his judgment" refers to *everyone*. I fear no one, for it no longer matters what you think, say, or do. What do your thoughts, words, or deeds have to do with me? Under the arch, there is no *me* that can be hurt because there is no guilt that demands I be punished, abused, rejected, or abandoned. Therefore I do not see you as punishing, abusing, rejecting, or abandoning *me*. Your wrong mind might be choosing victimization, and your body acting accordingly, but you are not doing this to *me*. The *you* who seems to attack is outside the arch, because you remain fearful of being under the arch with me.

That is what I know for everyone, including myself. Whatever our egos do, whatever our wrong mind would have us think or feel is irrelevant to who we truly are. Life under the arch includes everyone—no differences, no exceptions.

Again: "He does not fear his judgment for he has judged no one..." Because I have not judged you, I cannot perceive you as judging me. I therefore perceive your actions as having nothing to do with me, but everything to do with the decision you made to live outside the arch. My lack of judgment allows my love—the love of Jesus through me—to call to you to come home. That is what *A Course in Miracles* means in saying the Holy Spirit sees attack as fear, and fear as a call for love (T-12.I.8-10). Hearing everyone's call for love, we unify the dissonant voices of the world's symphony. Forgiveness dissolves its cacophony into the sweet calls for love others do not believe they deserve. Thus does everything change. The world does not change, but why should it? There *is* no world; it is the mind alone that needs changing.

(10:5) He does not fear his judgment for he has judged no one, nor has sought to be released through judgment from what judgment must impose.

Judgment imposes guilt and punishment, and the ego has us use judgment to escape from judgment:

judging others to escape from the judgment of ourselves. That is the hell of life outside the arch. I try to escape the judgment of my own guilt by putting it on you, attacking you for it. This only makes me guiltier, which means I expect you to judge and attack me back, reinforcing my judgment of myself that I need to project. Thus we go around and around the guilt-attack cycle that is the ego's bread and butter. Every war fought is the same as every other, because our personal wars never change. We have "sought to be released through judgment from what judgment must impose," and this is the hell to which we have all adjusted; so much so, in fact, that we think life outside the arch is reality.

To repeat, the question we need ask is why we would ever choose such a horrendous life. When we have allowed ourselves to hear love's melody at least once, even its faintest reminiscence, why would we choose anything else? All of us who work with this course hear that melody on some level; otherwise we would not be attracted to its words. It is the sound we listen to as we read. Even if we totally misinterpret the words, we yet feel a loving presence and hear its gentle sounds. Why would we give those up? That is the question Jesus repeatedly asks, and it is the question he wants us to ask ourselves each day.

(10:6) And all the while he is remembering what he forgot, when judgment seemed to be the way to save him from its penalty.

While we indulge the ego's dreams of judgment outside the arch, desperately trying to forget our Self, there is another part of our minds that remembers:

> Your other life has continued without interruption, and has been and always will be totally unaffected by your attempts to dissociate it (T-4.VI.1:7).

That is why the Holy Spirit is described as the memory of God, the present memory within (see T-28.I) that links us to what we have tried to forget, but just as fervently wish to remember. All we are asked to do—what it means to see our lives as classrooms—is learn how miserable we are when we step outside the arch of love and peace, and ask ourselves, to state this again, why we would ever make that choice. We need to ask that question without judgment and fear, recognizing that choosing life outside the arch makes us unhappy, and there is no one and nothing to blame for that unhappiness except ourselves. Returning to our right minds, we rest in silence within the safe pillars of Heaven's love, as reflected in this little poem of Helen's:

The Arch Of Silence

The love of Heaven arches over me
In perfect quiet. Nothing from the world
Can reach within its stillness. There can be
No sharp intruders and no witnesses
To unreality. The simple might
Of innocence alone is there. Pretense
Of any kind has fallen out of sight.
In honest clarity the world appears,
Redeemed and wakened from the dream of tears.

(*The Gifts of God*, p. 22)

5. Practical Applications of Forgiveness

Seeing Everyone as the Same

Q: This is about seeing everyone the same way you see Jesus and yourself. Intellectually, and sometimes in my practice, I can see the love in everyone, because I can at least imagine or have faith that behind the facade of the ego that I am seeing love is there. But how can I justify, even intellectually, seeing in Jesus the ugliness of Hitler?

A: The answer is you would not see it. As is said in the clarification of terms, Jesus is one who saw the face of Christ in his brother and remembered God (C-5.2:1), thus transcending the ego. The point of the principle is that if you judge a Hitler, are you willing to make the same judgment about Jesus? And the answer of course is "no." This then means that your judgment about Hitler—to use the overly simplistic twentieth-century symbol of evil incarnate—has to be false. The Holy Spirit's true perception—Christ's vision—does not judge differences or even see them. Eyes see differences and the wrong-minded thought system judges them. The right-minded thought system, however, sees differences but says: "So what!—these differences do not make a difference."

This clearly implies that the ego does not exist. Light abolishes darkness, love cancels fear, truth undoes illusion. When you bring guilt and forgiveness together, the guilt disappears and forgiveness is no longer needed. What remains is the blazing light of forgiveness (C-4.7:4), which opens our minds to knowledge, the Course's synonym for Heaven. Hitler and Jesus are thus the same because both are part of the same Sonship. The only difference is in time: one is awake, the other sleeps, dreaming of an illusory existence. Why, then, should we get upset about a person who does not exist? That would make us psychotic.

Q: Several years ago there was a widely reported case of a mother who drowned her two children. The reporters were asking everyone what they thought about it. I remember thinking to myself that there were times when I felt so angry and desperate with my kids that I wanted to kill them. I did not do it, but the thought certainly occurred in my mind that I was so mad I wanted to kill someone. That showed me that I am capable of the same thing. Is that how the process works?

A: Yes. The key to forgiveness—which means the key to practicing this course—is recognizing we are all the same. Everyone has the same wrong-minded thought system of guilt and hate. Not everyone would literally drown their children, but most people would kill if it meant preserving themselves.

When I was in college I worked in the psychology lab, and one of my jobs was to take care of the white rats that were used for experiments. I remember my horror one morning when I looked in a cage and saw lots of blood and fewer rats than were there the previous day. A mother rat had eaten some of the babies in her litter. My professor then explained to me that sometimes if the mother is not capable of taking care of her young she will eat them, because her instincts told her this is the most loving thing she can do. So, too, that poor woman who drowned her children must have unconsciously come to the same conclusion. That does not make her actions right-minded, of course, but it does provide a context in which we can understand what happened. Anytime you hurt someone, or concoct a plan as head of state to destroy another nation or ethnic/religious group, as insane and unloving as it is, there is still a method, referring to *Hamlet* once again, to the madness: the only way we believe we can survive, both as individuals as well as leaders of a country, is to destroy those we feel are threats to our existence.

We all do this because that is what we did at the beginning with God. His Love—perfect Oneness—was a threat to our individual identity. In the presence of that Oneness—reflected by life under the arch—our special identity would disappear. Any self-respecting ego must thus seek to destroy the threat, at least in the dream. We all carry with us the idea we have a mortal enemy, in whose presence we cannot exist. Since self-preservation is all-important, we have no recourse but to destroy this object of our projected hate. Some live this thought in socially unacceptable ways; others in socially acceptable ways, yet it remains present in everyone.

Therefore the key to learning this course is realizing we are all the same, as echoed in the New Year's prayer at the end of Chapter 15: "Make this year different by making it all the same" (T-15.XI.10:11). This means seeing everyone and every situation in the same way. That is the key. If we are the same, we all share the ego's wrong-minded thought system of guilt and hate, the Holy Spirit's right-minded thought system of forgiveness and love, and the power to choose between them. If we had this awareness of being alike, what could we attack? After all, we can attack only what we perceive as different. Why, then, do we attack? Because it is imperative that we perceive others as different. Behind every perception of differences is that another is guilty and we are not. This fulfills the ego's secret wish, the image that we want to be true (T-24.VII.8:10): we exist, but someone else is responsible. In order for that to be true, we *must* perceive differences: *you* the abuser, I the abused; *you* the victimizer; I the victim; *you* the oppressor, I the oppressed. We will never let these perceptions go, for that is what defines us and preserves our innocent self.

Helen once asked Jesus what she should say to someone in need of help—a seemingly right-minded question to ask, right? Wrong! Jesus replied that it was not the right question, the gist of which was: "Do not ask me what you should say. Ask instead for help to look through my eyes instead of the eyes of judgment. My eyes do not see differences; yours do. When you release the judgment—this person needs help from *you*, which reinforces distinctions rather than sameness—the love within, which embraces everyone, would flow unimpeded through you. Thus you will inevitably say whatever is helpful, realizing this love has nothing to do with the person or situation, but with Christ's vision that sees everyone living together under the arch." Thus Jesus says this course is simple —we are always practicing the single lesson of seeing everyone with the same split mind. We do not deny the ego in people, but we also do not deny it is a universal defense against the right mind that everyone has as well. And if there are right and wrong minds, there must be a part of the mind that chooses between them—the decision maker.

Q: To generalize, I hear you saying that when we define ourselves as a victim of others, we are abusing them. So in making Hitler the bad guy, I am abusing the concentration camp.

A: Yes. It is abusive because you say to the victims: "You poor dears; you are stuck in this world, innocent victims of what these terrible people are doing to you." In truth, they are not poor, poor dears, but powerful minds who have so chosen, and thus can choose again. As we read in the workbook, of one who lives a victimized life outside the arch:

> Yet is he really tragic, when you see that he is following the way he chose, and need but realize Who walks with him and open up his treasures to be free? (W-pI.166.6:3)

Another's tragic "fate" has nothing to do with you, and if you think it does, you but do what Jesus told Helen he would not do: depreciate the power of her mind to choose to be in a state of fear. If he took the fear away from her, thus identifying with her abused self, he would be depreciating the power of her mind that chose this dream. Jesus thus says to us: "The only way I can help is to remind you of your mind's power to dream, then show you the dream. When you look at it with me, you will say, 'I do not want to do that again; it is too hurtful,' and will then automatically choose the Holy Spirit."

This idea, though in different words, is also expressed in "True Empathy" (T-16.I). The problem with the world's empathy is that we empathize with only *part* of the Sonship—the innocent victims. We are thus unknowingly weakening the Sonship by depreciating the power of its mind. True empathy sees the strength of Christ in everyone, which means the strength of the mind to choose Christ's strength or choose against it—the ego. True empathy sees everyone as the same, victim and victimizer, weak and strong, abused and abuser.

Thus, though we do what normal people do on the level of *form,* on the level of *content*—the mind—we do not judge. Everyone calls for help, the so-called weak and the so-called strong, because all think they are bodies, stuck in a dream they did not make—fraught with pain and ending in death—over which they have no control. What a dreadful situation for people to be in! And everyone *is* in it, for the world lives outside the arch, wandering "uncertain, lonely and in constant fear" (T-31.VIII.7:1)—good guys and bad guys. We are all such wanderers because this world is not our home. Fear of God's punishment drove us from the mind into the world, which is why Jesus asks us not to make a judgment we would not generalize to all people.

Forgiveness in the Work Place

Q: There's a man at work who is like the town crier —he loves to talk badly about everyone. Not very many people come into my office and sit down and talk to me, so when he comes in, I'm happy to have him pull up a chair. Yet it feels like he is spreading poison. There are times when I don't like it and times when I do. I do not really want to stop him from coming in and talking to me, but is there a "good" way I can be with him and listen to him? Since this is a work relationship, I want to stay on good terms with him.

A: Why don't you just love him? No one would walk around bad-mouthing people unless he felt terrible about himself. So when he is sitting there, why don't you go beyond his words to the pain he must be feeling, and let your heart go out to him? Make him right; don't make him wrong.

Q: Okay, but one other thing about this situation. There is one person whom he talks really badly about, and the other day someone told me such good things about this same person.

A: Perception lies, right? Obviously, the person that said the bad things is lying, as is the person who said the good things. They are all lying. Therefore, just make this person right. As you see this going on in your office, feel the pain that has to be there. People could not attack anyone if they came from a place of love inside. And so if someone is attacking, as this man seems always to do, he obviously is not coming from a loving space. There is no other alternative. If love is not present, then hate, guilt, and pain must be. Feel his pain, and let him know he is right and that you accept him. All he wants is to be accepted, to have someone say to him: "You're okay." That is all. Simply tell him: "You know something? You're okay." That's the message you give, regardless of your words. On a larger scale, no heads of state could make a decision that adversely affected so many millions of people unless they were in deep pain, and thought in their insanity that the only way to escape from this terrible self-loathing is to beat up on some group halfway around the world. The pain is there, no matter what side of the political fence you are on. The political party does not matter, because *everyone* comes from the same split mind.

Now that you have mastered that, we are ready to take another step. You have to do this with *everyone*. Practice with this man; but once you see how well it works, how good it makes you feel, how good it makes *him* feel, ask yourself: "Why can't I do this with everyone? What stops me from feeling everyone's pain?" Don't force yourself to do it with everyone, but just stop and think about why you would choose against such happiness and joy. And as you practice with one situation and see how well it works, look in the mirror and do the same thing with yourself. The parts of you that you find abhorrent and do not like are also coming from this place of deep pain. Again, there is not one of us walking this earth who does not experience the pain of self-hatred, born of the idea that we destroyed Heaven's love and thus will never be able to return to it. And even if we could, the door would be forever closed to us.

Therefore, practice with certain people in your life and see how the love your forgiveness expressed would naturally extend to everyone, and then see how you seek to prevent its flow. Watch how you pick and choose, believing that some are easier to forgive than others. Start with the "easy" ones, but recognize that if you really wish to feel good within yourself, be healed, and awaken from the dream, you must allow your non-judgmental acceptance to embrace all people. Finally, forgive yourself when you say you will let the grievance go here, but not there.

Make everyone right because everyone is right. Everyone is also wrong, but don't say that. People may not be right on the level of form, yet on the level of content you make them right, which means you understand where they are coming from and you do not judge. If you are teaching children arithmetic, for example, and they say 2 + 2 is 7, you are not helping them if you say: "That is a brilliant answer." You can correct the form by still making the children right. If you are running an office and people make mistakes, you may certainly point out the errors and try to help them be avoided. People do make mistakes—indeed, bodies were made to make mistakes—and there is a way of pointing these out that is hateful, humiliating, and punitive, and a way that is loving, kind, and gentle. The latter makes people right as Sons of God who have simply made a mistake.

Who, then, does not fall into that category of being wrong? We are all Sons of God who made a mistake in the beginning by betting on the wrong horse. As one Son we placed our bet, and it bankrupted us. As I once said in a workshop, we bet on a horse that dropped dead in the starting gate, and yet we still ride the same horse, beating it and trying to get it to run, while it goes nowhere. We are so blind that we think the horse is actually moving. Again, *all* of us have done the same thing. Our task, therefore, is to tell people they are right as Sons of God, and not terrible sinners because they made a mistake. Sometimes our content of forgiveness corrects the form; other times it is more important to let the form of the mistake pass. When our minds are free of conflict, we would automatically know what to do, and so there is nothing in this course that would tell us how to behave. Jesus does tell us, however, Whom we should bring with us into the office, the classroom, and everywhere else. If we have invited the Holy Spirit, we will not act out of anger or judgmental thoughts, regardless of our behavioral responses.

Helen had a good friend from graduate school whom she asked to serve as a consultant for an institute for retarded children with which Helen was involved, a position that required her to write a report important to the organization. However, when Helen read the final report she was horrified to find how terrible it was. Her friend, an otherwise excellent if not brilliant psychologist, had obviously not given it much attention. Helen was all set to tell her friend off, but decided first to ask Jesus what she should do. His answer was for Helen to rewrite the report and never tell her friend. In other words, to make her right but correct the mistake because Helen did not want to hurt the institute of which she was so fond. Helen thus rewrote the report and the friend never knew.

While this was an example where the error was corrected behind the scenes and the woman never knew, it certainly could have been that the most loving thing would have been to tell her, so she herself could correct the error. There is no right or wrong way of proceeding in terms of *form*, which always depends on the circumstance and situation, but the *content* of love is constant. To ensure that the form is loving, you have to be willing not to make the other person wrong.

If you come from the non-judgmental space under the arch, you will inevitably know the best and most loving intervention.

In *A Course in Miracles*, Jesus tells us we are both right *and* wrong. Yet when he points out our mistakes, it is never with the sense of attack or judgment. When he simply says, "You are wrong," his overriding content is "You are right." In the section "The Correction of Error" (T-9.III), he teaches that our function is to tell our brothers they are right, even though they may be temporarily insane. This has nothing to do with words, but with the attitude of non-condemnation. We do not judge others as egos, which would clearly make them wrong; we merely accept and respect them for who they are—the Son of God who is always right, even when he chooses wrongly.

Q: There would seem to be a built-in conflict: whether the relationship with the people is more important or the business doing well.

A: If you find the conflict unresolveable, it means there is a conflict in you that is unresolveable. It is certainly true that on one level there is tension between preventing the business from failing and valuing relationships; i.e., running the business so that no one loses and everyone gains. If you focus only on the relationships in the sense that you ignore everything else and the business fails, again, everyone loses. However, if there is no conflict within you, you will know exactly how to handle the business *and* relationships. Uncertainty therefore reflects that there is something unhealed in you. This, then, is your signal to go within and ask Jesus for help.

If you are not sure what to do, do not do anything. If the situation demands that you do something immediately, simply do the best you can. However, again, be aware that if you were conflict-free, you would know exactly what to do or say, and what business decisions to make that would not hurt others. To repeat the point, *if you are conflicted in terms of behavior, it is always because there is conflict in the mind.* This is the value the situation has for your healing; a red flag that says: "There is something unhealed within; otherwise I would know what to say and what to do." Thus you are able to ask for help to look at the situation differently, learn about your "secret sins and hidden hates" (T-31.VIII.9:2), and, most importantly, forgive yourself for not acting in an ego-free way.

The little willingness asked of us expresses the process of acknowledging that if we are upset or conflicted about anything, it is not because of the situation, relationship, or our bodily state, but because our minds have chosen to be outside the arch. We therefore ask Jesus for help to look at our world through his eyes, which look only within and never without. Our strong resistance to being wrong makes this far more difficult than it has to be. From Jesus' perspective, the body was made to say that we are right and God is wrong, for His very Being asserts there is no separation, and therefore no world. The body says, on the other hand: "I'll show you. Here is a world in which bodies suffer and die." This, then, is the body's purpose: to say, "I am right and you are wrong"; the *you* being Jesus, his course, and even God Himself. Thus the outcome is that whenever we are sure we are right about something, we are wrong, illustrating that the body and world were made to keep us as far away as possible from the arch of forgiveness and Atonement.

Q: My boss John is kind and intelligent, much more so than his right-hand man, Mike, who is my supervisor. I perceive a weakness in John, in that he is not firm enough and seems afraid of his authority. Mike tries to usurp him behind his back—usually with little things. I wish John would become stronger, because it would make him a better boss and it would be better for the company if he did not let the other man take over.

The other day John took his first day off in years. Mike immediately called a staff meeting in John's office and made a personnel announcement that was totally out of place. We all felt very uncomfortable. One of the other workers took pictures and e-mailed them to John, showing Mike in John's chair, sharing all this information with us. The e-mail was meant as a joke, but it was really more than that. John laughed, and asked Mike, whom he really trusts, what he had talked about in the meeting. Mike lied to him and attacked John. I wanted to help in some way, but I did not know how because John is totally unaware of Mike's dishonesty. I am waiting for the right moment to bring it up. Should an employee go to the boss and tell him what went on in his absence, and can I tell John without hurting anyone?

A: The problem is that you are not talking about "poor Mike." This whole story is about "poor John." How about "poor Mike"? Why would anyone try to usurp his boss' place unless he felt overwhelmed with guilt? Think about "poor Mike," and then you will know what to do about "poor John."

To expand on this answer, what often happens in families, including those who work with them, is that people choose up sides. Invariably they choose to identify with the victim—child or spouse—with the abuser seen as the enemy. That is exactly what the ego thrives on—making a judgment about one person that you would not make about everyone. You side with the abused because they have been abused by someone else, and in so doing you are really abusing the abuser, ending up being part of the same problem you are trying to correct.

This is a major issue in every situation—in the home, office, psychotherapy, etc.: *What about poor Mike?* Think about him. In your mind he is the usurper, which means he is the one who usurped God's place. It was not poor John or poor you. It was Mike! You now tell God/John that you found out who did it. Pointedly, you are making a judgment about one person that you would not make about everyone. Needless to say, it is difficult to avoid this, especially where there is a situation of clear abuse. Yet if healing is to occur, you must ask Jesus' help to rise above these judgments to make his one judgment: all God's Sons are both abused and abusers, and behind this insanity is their inherent oneness as God's innocent Son.

All of us here are miserable, living in this terrible world that is not our home. Jesus tells us the body is a "travesty" of who we are (T-24.VII.10:9), a "rotting prison" (T-26.I.8:3) in which we feel trapped. Since we all have bodies, we cope as best we can. As we have seen, some cope in socially acceptable ways, others in socially unacceptable ways. Yet no one is truly different from another. On a practical level, *true perception* does not mean seeing the light of Christ in everyone, the attempt that often lends itself to denial. Instead, we first see that all people have the same ego, struggling with the same insane thought system and hopeless despair from which they will never escape. Given this thought system, a concept of hell is inevitable. Regardless of our religious beliefs, we believe in hell because this world is hell. How could a world outside God's Love be anything else? Thus we ask Jesus to help us let the veils fall from our eyes, that we would come to see everyone as the same. Scratch beneath the surface of even the most wicked person and you will see a frightened child. People could not possibly attack another unless they felt vulnerable inside. No matter how much they bluster and justify their actions, they could not hurt anyone, whether an individual or group, unless they first felt hurt, damaged, and terrified.

Practicing this course, therefore, means seeing everyone as the same. Rather than housing the secret wish to keep the separation and blame everyone else for it, we now want the right-minded wish of being proven wrong and seeing the inherent sameness in all people; and then forgiving ourselves when we do not.

Q: As a corollary to this, what about the dilemma of being a whistle blower? Young people seem to run into the dilemma of whether or not to tell on a friend involved with drugs, for example.

A: The course does not take a position on this specific form, for the only whistle blowing you should do is on the ego—the thought of separation taken seriously. When, through judgment, you separate yourself from certain people, you are merely telling them they are right about taking separation seriously; there are good people and bad people, and you are going to blow the whistle on the bad ones. Yet, the only one you should blow the whistle on is yourself, for thinking there is someone you should blow the whistle on. Again, blow the whistle on the ego—*everyone's* ego—and even more to the point, blow it on *all* people's decision maker that chose the ego, and then conveniently forgot what they chose.

Jesus would tell us to come to him first—above the battleground of the world—and let him help us look at the situation in which everyone is the same. Perhaps the most loving thing would be to blow the whistle, or perhaps to walk away and do nothing. Jesus would not say that whistle blowing is good or bad; besides, you cannot decide for another anyway. All you can do is present a model to the teenager—to use your example—of someone who does not judge. They will either choose to emulate you or go against you. Needless to say, on the level of form you do judge, for this is inevitable with bodies. Yet you need not make a judgment based on separation or attack. We differentiate on the level of form, but not content, for everyone shares the same split mind.

Q: Sometimes I am trying to apply the Course at work and then something like this happens: My executive director will have an issue with someone that is pure attack. I feel like I don't get it because I'm not in that place of attack. She responds angrily with: "Are you, crazy? Can't you see this?" And I want to say "No, we're both insane, because we could see it totally differently if we wanted to."

A: My answer is similar to my comments earlier: *make her right*. The challenge is not to tell others they are wrong. Rather, the challenge here might be to act as if you are seeing it the way your director is, and even to *behave* as if you are seeing it that way, but without taking it seriously. In other words, you want to be able to live in a battleground such as business, and yet be peaceful. Do what others do on the battleground; otherwise you are not going to be successful. But be peaceful. That would make you a much better teacher for your colleagues, as well as for yourself. This is much better than preaching, although I am not suggesting that you are. Instead of accentuating the differences between you and others, it may be more loving to join with them on the level of *form* and let the *content* of peace, love, and the vision of oneness gently come through you. That does not happen in one day, but over a period of time it will make a big difference—not only for you, but for others as well.

It is unlikely that the world of business is going to change, any more than the political process in the world's countries will change. However, what can change is your reaction to them. That is all you need be concerned about. If there is external change, it is basically irrelevant. There may indeed be substantial change in the future, but what is truly important is that *you* change; that you be at peace early in the morning, as you go to work, at work, on your way home, and into the evening. You increasingly see that this is the only purpose of being an executive; not to make a lot of money, run a successful company and bury the opposition, but to be peaceful and right-minded throughout, and on the level of content, not to see your interests as separate from anyone else's, even though on the behavioral level they most certainly are. The challenge, therefore, is not to change behavior or externals, but to change how you look at them: "Seek not to change the world, but choose to change your mind about the world" (T-21.in.1:7); seek not to change your business, but choose to change your mind about your business. From that change of mind, many things may happen. Yet again, all that matters is that you have done your part in changing your mind.

Try to see each day as a way of gathering information about yourself as you are being a normal executive, doing your job as best you can. Try to be aware of how quickly you forget what you are learning, whether you are doing the workbook, reading the text, or simply thinking about it. Even while you are on the battleground of the corporate world, with bombs dropping all around you—the world of *kill or be killed*—your experience will be different because you will not be taking it quite as seriously as you used to. As you walk the path of business, you will know you also walk a right-minded path. Over time this will become much more important to you and more prominent in your awareness than what you are actually doing in your office. In the end, it will make you much more effective in business, too, because you will have less tension, anger, and conflict, which only cloud your vision and distort your judgment. You may look like every other person in business, but as the workbook says, there will be something different about you—you will smile more frequently (W-pI.155.1). You will not be so angry, guilty, depressed, stressed, anxious, or fearful.

This, then, is applicable to any role or relationship, whether a parent, friend, employer, or employee. You undo the disassociation of being one person at home and another at work. Again, you do not necessarily change the *form*, although the form may certainly change at some point. You change the *content*, as Jesus becomes for you a symbol of what it means to live under the arch of forgiveness: the perfect integration of form and content.

Q: I am not sure of what to do when people in my office gang up on another person. It happens often. I don't want to join in the attack, but when I don't, I feel like I'm separate.

A: This is similar to the earlier question, and there is no right or wrong answer on the form level, as we just considered. Yet there is an ideal you want to aspire to in your mind: the vision that everyone is the same, and that you do not wish to act in any way that makes differences real. Therefore, before you have a feel for what to do on the level of behavior, begin with the premise that *everyone* in the situation is wrong—victims and victimizers. Everyone is wrong, and you are wrong, too, if you think there is a good and bad. If you feel bad for the person being scapegoated, you inevitably scapegoat the scapegoaters. If you ally with the scapegoaters against the "scapegoatee," you are still making separation and differences real. On the level of form, it is impossible not to have preferences and join with some groups and not others. Yet there remains a way of joining that is not joining *against*.

While you cannot behaviorally include all people all the time—you cannot have lunch with everyone, for example—you can include everyone on the level of thought, in the sense of not attacking or judging others.

Perhaps the most loving thing is to join the scapegoaters, because you do not want to be separate from them, telling them they are right; perhaps it is to say the same thing to the scapegoatee, putting your arm around him or her in comfort; or perhaps it is not to participate at all. While there is no right or wrong behavior, there is a right or wrong perception: seeing people as the same is of the Holy Spirit, while seeing everyone as different is of the ego. When you have no investment in one group or the other, you will automatically do or say whatever is the most loving. If you do not, that is helpful information you just learned about yourself; that you are still gripped by guilt and fear, and are attempting to make the separation real.

In other words, the best way of handling situations like this, once they arise, is to see them as your classrooms—laboratories in which you practice what you are learning; opportunities to forgive yourself if you have not learned the lesson because your guilt and anger impelled you to choose up sides. These situations thus offer you the chance to feel happy that you are making progress, realizing that the way you handled the situation today is much different from how you handled it before. Even if your response is as it once was, you at least know what you are doing.

Q: Is it really a matter of pulling back and saying, "I see this happening and have these feelings. Jesus, take them from me and fix the situation"?

A: No, Jesus cannot take them from you unless you give them to him. Recall how he had told Helen that she should not ask him what she should say to someone, but rather to ask his help to let go of her judgments. The implication was that you would then automatically say what would be the most helpful. Jesus does not deal with the body, because there is no body. Everything in the world of form is a projection of the mind's thoughts. *Everything*. The fundamental principle governing the Course's thought system is *ideas leave not their source*—the principle of the Atonement that says the separation never happened, and so there is no external world. Therefore, Jesus would say: "Why are you asking me to fix a situation, or to tell you what to say when ideas leave not their source? There is no world out there, since it has never left its source in your mind. It is in the mind that you will find me, a loving presence to which you bring your darkened thoughts of guilt and judgment."

Thus, when you find yourself in an office situation where there is backbiting, anger, if not outright malevolence, and you are tempted to make judgments of a group or yourself for judging, you need to bring those judgments to the egoless presence of light and love in your mind. That is all. To the extent to which you bring the darkness of your specialness to the light, the darkness will disappear, and abstract love will flow through your mind into the specific body. Anything you think, feel, say, or do will inevitably express that love. Thus, your task is to bring the interference to the principle of non-interference, the meaning of asking Jesus for help. Again, the focus is not on asking him to fix a situation or to tell you what to do—which job you should take, house you should buy, relationship you should be in, or what words you should use—because *ideas leave not their source*.

The ego's principle, on which its thought system rests, is that ideas *do* leave their source. Why, then, would you want to ask Jesus to help you uphold a principle that categorically goes against everything he teaches? Yet this is what you do by asking him to depreciate the power of your mind or help with something external. It is a gross misreading of everything in this course to think that this is its focus. To restate this important point, the Course's fundamental teaching is that *ideas leave not their source*: the thought of separation never left the mind to make a world of separation. Therefore, what has to be healed is the mind that believed the impossible could happen.

"I Am Here Only to Be Truly Helpful"

At this point I should like to review a prayer from the early part of the text: "I am here only to be truly helpful" (T-2.V.18). It was originally part of a personal message for Bill, which did not belong in the Course itself since it was specific to a particular situation. We took the message out, but kept this prayer because it was so lovely. I will start with its introduction:

> You can do much on behalf of your own healing and that of others if, in a situation calling for help, you think of it this way:
>
> *I am here only to be truly helpful.*
> *I am here to represent Him Who sent me.*
> *I do not have to worry about what to say or what to do, because He Who sent me will direct me.*
> *I am content to be wherever He wishes, knowing He goes there with me.*
> *I will be healed as I let him teach me to heal.*

This prayer can be misleading if we confuse *form* and *content*. Yet its meaning is clear from what follows, not to mention Jesus' message to Helen about not looking through the eyes of judgment. The two sections in Chapter 2 that come next also make clear that Jesus is not talking about behavior. In fact, he gently chides Helen, as the reader may recall, for asking him to take away her fear of something external, saying, in effect: "Do not ask me to remove your fear, but instead let me help you with the conditions of the mind that led to it—your willingness to be separate" (T-2.VI.4:3-4).

This prayer, therefore, is a wonderful expression of what we have been discussing; specifically, finding oneself in a situation that calls for help. Combining this prayer with other concepts in *A Course in Miracles*, we realize that what is helpful—*the only thing that is helpful*—is to remind people they can make another choice. This is the only true help we can be to anyone, the meaning of living with Jesus under his arch. Thus, in the midst of a conflicted situation, we strive to be a presence that says to *all* people: "My brother, choose again. Choose a thought system that does not see separate but only shared interests." Everyone is calling for help—victims and victimizers, good guys and bad guys, scapegoatees and scapegoaters—for we are all in the same ego boat. Extending help means manifesting the peace that comes only from being in the right mind, reminding others that the holy instant we have chosen is the same one they can choose—right-mindedness instead of wrong-mindedness. The former always sees separate interests, makes distinctions, and perceives differences as justifiable and valid; the latter sees in everyone the universal call for help and its universal answer. In other words, right-minded thinking does not acknowledge the concept *difference*, only *sameness*.

Understanding this will help us not fall into the form-content trap in reading this prayer. *"I am here only to be truly helpful. I am here to represent Him Who sent me"* does not mean that Jesus or the Holy Spirit send people to us, although that is our experience, as it was Helen's and Bill's. Yet how could They really send people to us? There are no people to send! Jesus and the Holy Spirit are not involved in the world of form, and yet we keep trying to drag Them into our insanity so that They would share it. We do this because we think that if They join our insanity, we would become sane. Therefore, not only do Jesus and the Holy Spirit not send people, They do not do anything at all, being only a Presence of right-minded and loving thinking in our dream. Since this dream is in the mind and not the body, it is to Their loving Presence that we bring our unloving thoughts, returning from the ego's world to Jesus' world, to live gratefully at last within the pillars of his loving arch.

6. Conclusion

I close with Helen's poem, "The Soundless Song." One sentence in particular blends beautifully with our discussion: "And I lean on Him in sure / Unswerving confidence." We are asked to lean on Christ's pillar in "sure unswerving confidence," and this gives us the strength to become that pillar, as each of us in turn becomes His constant comfort for others. Yet this cannot happen unless we grow, unless we have someone to grow with, happily represented for us by Jesus. We therefore need to see the purpose of each day as moving closer and closer to Jesus' pillar of love, for this alone gives meaning to our lives, now lived under his arch of forgiveness and peace.

The Soundless Song

I walk in stillness. Where my rest is set
Is Heaven. And the silence of the stars
Sings in a soundless circle. For the song
Of Heaven is past hearing, and ascends
Beyond the tiny range the ear can catch,
And soars into a spaceless magnitude
Where sound and silence meet in unity.

Holy am I, who brings my Father's Name
With me and who abides in Him, although
I seem to walk alone. Look carefully,
And you may catch a glimpse of Him who stands
Beside me. And I lean on Him in sure
Unswerving confidence. It was not thus
Before, for I was bitterly afraid
To take the Help of Heaven for my own.
Yet Heaven never failed, and only I
Stayed comfortless, while all of Heaven's gifts
Poured out before me. Now the arms of Christ
Are all I have and all my treasure is.
Now I have ceased to question. Now I come
From chaos to the stillness of my home.

(*The Gifts of God*, p. 76)

INDEX OF REFERENCES TO *A COURSE IN MIRACLES*

text

text (cont.)

workbook for students

manual for teachers

clarification of terms

Psychotherapy: Purpose, Process and Practice

The Song of Prayer

The Gifts of God

Foundation for A Course in Miracles

Kenneth Wapnick *received his Ph.D. in Clinical Psychology in 1968 from Adelphi University. He was a close friend and associate of Helen Schucman and William Thetford, the two people whose joining together was the immediate stimulus for the scribing of A Course in Miracles. Kenneth has been involved with A Course in Miracles since 1973, writing, teaching, and integrating its principles with his practice of psychotherapy. He is on the Executive Board of the Foundation for Inner Peace, publishers of A Course in Miracles.*

In 1983, with his wife Gloria, he began the Foundation for A Course in Miracles, and in 1984 this evolved into a Teaching and Healing Center in Crompond, New York, which was quickly outgrown. In 1988 they opened the Academy and Retreat Center in upstate New York. In 1995 they began the Institute for Teaching Inner Peace through A Course in Miracles, an educational corporation chartered by the New York State Board of Regents. In 2001 the Foundation moved to Temecula, California, and shifted its emphasis to electronic teaching. The Foundation publishes a quarterly newsletter, "The Lighthouse," which is available free of charge. The following is Kenneth's and Gloria's vision of the Foundation.

In our early years of studying *A Course in Miracles,* as well as teaching and applying its principles in our respective professions of psychotherapy, and teaching and school administration, it seemed evident that this was not the simplest of thought systems to understand. This was so not only in the intellectual grasp of its teachings, but perhaps more importantly in the application of these teachings to our personal lives. Thus, it appeared to us from the beginning that the Course lent itself to teaching, parallel to the ongoing teachings of the Holy Spirit in the daily opportunities within our relationships, which are discussed in the early pages of the manual for teachers.

One day several years ago while Helen Schucman and I (Kenneth) were discussing these ideas, she shared a vision that she had had of a teaching center as a white temple with a gold cross atop it. Although it was clear that this image was symbolic, we understood it to be representative of what the teaching center was to be: a place where the person of Jesus and his message in *A Course in Miracles* would be manifest. We have sometimes seen an image of a lighthouse shining its light into the sea, calling to it those passers-by who sought it. For us, this light is the Course's teaching of forgiveness, which we would hope to share with those who are drawn to the Foundation's form of teaching and its vision of *A Course in Miracles.*

This vision entails the belief that Jesus gave the Course at this particular time in this particular form for several reasons. These include:

1) the necessity of healing the mind of its belief that attack is salvation; this is accomplished through forgiveness, the undoing of our belief in the reality of separation and guilt.

2) emphasizing the importance of Jesus and/or the Holy Spirit as our loving and gentle Teacher, and developing a personal relationship with this Teacher.

3) correcting the errors of Christianity, particularly where it has emphasized suffering, sacrifice, separation, and sacrament as being inherent in God's plan for salvation.

Our thinking has always been inspired by Plato (and his mentor Socrates), both the man and his teachings. Plato's Academy was a place where serious and thoughtful people came to study his philosophy in an atmosphere conducive to their learning, and then returned to their professions to implement what they were taught by the great philosopher. Thus, by integrating abstract philosophical ideals with experience, Plato's school seemed to be the perfect model for the teaching center that we directed for so many years.

We therefore see the Foundation's principal purpose as being to help students of *A Course in Miracles* deepen their understanding of its thought system, conceptually and experientially, so that they may be more effective instruments of Jesus' teaching in their own lives. Since teaching forgiveness without experiencing it is empty, one of the Foundation's specific goals is to help facilitate the process whereby people may be better able to know that their own sins are forgiven and that they are truly loved by God. Thus is the Holy Spirit able to extend His Love through them to others.

Responding in part to the "electronic revolution," we have taken the Foundation's next step in our move to Temecula, California. With this move to a non-residential setting we are shifting our focus, though not exclusively, from totally live presentations to electronic and digital forms of teaching in order to maximize the benefits of the burgeoning field of electronic media communication. This will allow us to increase our teaching outreach, the *content* of which will remain the same, allowing its *form* to adapt to the 21st century.

Related Material on *A Course in Miracles*

By Kenneth Wapnick, Ph.D.

Books

(For a complete list and full descriptions of our books and audio and video publications, please see our Web site at www.facim.org, or call or write for our free catalog.)

Christian Psychology in *A Course in Miracles*. Second edition, enlarged.
ISBN 0-933291-14-0 • #B-1 • Paperback • 90 pages $5
Audio version of the second edition of the book, read by Kenneth Wapnick • #T2 $10

Translation available in Spanish.

A Talk Given on *A Course in Miracles*: An Introduction. Seventh edition.
ISBN 0-933291-16-7 • #B-3 • Paperback • 131 pages $6

Translations available in Spanish, Portuguese, German, Dutch, French, Danish, Italian, Slovene, and Afrikaans.

Glossary-Index for *A Course in Miracles*. Fifth edition, revised and enlarged.
ISBN 0-933291-03-5 • #B-4 • Paperback • 349 pages $10

Translations available in Spanish and *German.*

Forgiveness and Jesus: The Meeting Place of *A Course in Miracles* and Christianity. Sixth edition.
ISBN 0-933291-13-2 • #B-5 • Paperback • 399 pages $16

Translations available in Spanish and German.

The Fifty Miracle Principles of *A Course in Miracles*. Fifth edition.
ISBN 0-933291-15-9 • #B-6 • Paperback • 107 pages $8

Translations available in Spanish and German.

Awaken from the Dream. Second edition. Gloria and Kenneth Wapnick.
ISBN 0-933291-04-3 • #B-7 • Paperback • 132 pages $10

Translations available in German and Spanish.

The Obstacles to Peace.
ISBN 0-933291-05-1 • #B-8 • Paperback • 295 pages $12

Love Does Not Condemn: The World, the Flesh, and the Devil According to Platonism, Christianity, Gnosticism, and *A Course in Miracles*.
ISBN 0-933291-07-8 • #B-9 • Hardcover • 614 pages $25

A Vast Illusion: Time According to *A Course in Miracles*. Second edition.
ISBN 0-933291-09-4 • #B-10 • Paperback • 345 pages $12

Translation available in German.

Absence from Felicity: The Story of Helen Schucman and Her Scribing of *A Course in Miracles*. Second edition.
ISBN 0-933291-08-6 • #B-11 • Paperback • 498 pages $17

Translation available in German.

Overeating: A Dialogue. An Application of the Principles of *A Course in Miracles*. Second edition.
ISBN 0-933291-11-6 • #B-12 • Paperback • 70 pages $5

***A Course in Miracles* and Christianity: A Dialogue.**
Kenneth Wapnick and W. Norris Clarke, S.J.
ISBN 0-933291-18-3 • #B-13 • Paperback • 110 pages $7

Translations available in Spanish and German.

The Most Commonly Asked Questions About *A Course in Miracles*. Gloria and Kenneth Wapnick.
ISBN 0-933291-21-3 • #B-14 • Paperback • 144 pages $8

Translations available in Spanish, German, and Dutch.

The Message of *A Course in Miracles*. Volume One: *All Are Called*. Volume Two: *Few Choose to Listen*.
Two Volumes: 619 pages
ISBN 0-933291-25-6 • #B-15 • Paperback $22 (set)

Translations available in Spanish and German.

The Journey Home: "The Obstacles to Peace" in *A Course in Miracles*.
ISBN 0-933291-24-8 • #B-16 • Paperback • 510 pages $16.95

Ending Our Resistance to Love: The Practice of *A Course in Miracles*.
ISBN 1-59142-132-2 • #B-17 • Paperback • 94 pages $5.00

Life, Death, and Love: Shakespeare's Great Tragedies and *A Course in Miracles*. Four-volume set based on *King Lear, Hamlet, Macbeth,* and *Othello*.
Four Volumes: 383 pages
ISBN 1-59142-142-X • #B-18 • Paperback $25 (set)

The Healing Power of Kindness—Volume One: Releasing Judgment.
ISBN 1-59142-147-0 • #B19 • Paperback • 109 pages $6.00

The Healing Power of Kindness—Volume Two: Forgiving Our Limitations.
ISBN 1-59142-155-1 • #B20 • Paperback • 118 pages $6.00

Form versus Content: Sex and Money.
ISBN 1-59142-194-2 • #B-21 • Paperback • 116 pages $7.00

Journey through the Workbook of *A Course in Miracles*. Commentary on the 365 lessons.
Eight Volumes: 1,158 pages
ISBN 1-59142-206-X • #B-23 • Paperback $60 (set)

Ordering Information

For orders ***in the continental U.S. only***, please add $6.00 for the first item, and $1.00 for each additional item, for shipping and handling. The shipping charge for *Journey through the Workbook of A Course in Miracles* is $10.00; add $1.00 for each additional item.

For orders to ***all other countries*** (SURFACE MAIL), and to ***Alaska, Hawaii***, and ***Puerto Rico*** (FIRST CLASS MAIL), please add $6.00 for the first item and $2.00 for each additional item. The shipping charge for *Journey through the Workbook of A Course in Miracles* is $10.00; add $2.00 for each additional item.

California State residents please add local sales tax.

VISA, MasterCard, Discover, American Express accepted.

Order from:

Foundation for A Course in Miracles
Dept. B
41397 Buecking Drive
Temecula, CA 92590
(951) 296-6261 • FAX (951) 296-5455
Visit our Web site at *www.facim.org*

* * * * *

To order additional copies of this book, send a check or money order (in US funds only) for $7.00 plus shipping to the above address; please see shipping charges above.

A Course in Miracles and other scribed material
may be ordered from:

Foundation for Inner Peace
P.O. Box 598
Mill Valley, CA 94942
(415) 388-2060

A Course in Miracles, Second Edition, Complete:
Hardcover - 6" x 9": $35
Softcover - 6" x 9": $30
Paperback - 5" x 8": $20

Psychotherapy: Purpose, Process and Practice: $6

The Song of Prayer: Prayer, Forgiveness, Healing: $6

The Gifts of God: $21

Concordance of *A Course in Miracles*: $49.95

Place
postage
here

Foundation for A Course in Miracles®
Dept. B
41397 Buecking Drive
Temecula, CA 92590

- [ ] I am interested in receiving a newsletter
- [ ] I am interested in receiving a catalog of books and tapes
- [ ] I am interested in receiving a schedule of workshops and classes
- [ ] Place me on your mailing list to receive your annual catalog and quarterly newsletter

PLEASE PRINT NEATLY

Name ______________________________

Address ______________________________

____

City, State, Zip ______________________________